Edited by
Lesley Abbott *and*
Rosemary Rodger

05

5

Open University Press
Buckingham · Philadelphia

To the children, staff and parents with whom
we talked, worked and played and from whom
we learned so much.

Open University Press
Celtic Court
22 Ballmoor
Buckingham
MK18 1XW

email: enquiries@openup.co.uk
world wide web: http://www.openup.co.uk

and
325 Chestnut Street
Philadelphia, PA 19106, USA

First Published 1994
Reprinted 1995, 1997, 2000

Copyright © The editors and contributors 1994

A catalogue record of this book is available from the British Library

ISBN   0 335 19230 0 (pb)   0 335 19231 9 (hb)

Library of Congress Cataloguing-in-Publication Data
Quality eduation in the early years / edited by Lesley Abbott,
    Rosemary Rodger.
        p. cm.
    Includes bibliographical references and index.
    ISBN 0–335–19231–9 (hb). — ISBN 0–335–19230–0 (pb)
    1. Early childhood education—Great Britain.   I. Abbott, Lesley,
    1945– .   II. Rodger, Rosemary, 1946–
LB1139.3.G7Q35   1994
372.21´0941—dc20   94–16355
                                                            CIP

Typeset by Graphicraft Ltd, Hong Kong
Printed in Great Britain by Biddles Ltd, www.biddles.co.uk

37, 38,
42, 49

Contents

iv   Contents

The contributors

All of the contributors to this book work together in the School of Education, the Manchester Metropolitan University.
Lesley Abbott is a principal lecturer and head of the Early Years team. She has taught across the primary age range, particularly in nursery and infant education. She has responsibility for early years teacher education at pre-service and in-service levels, together with multiprofessional developments within the School of Education. She is responsible for liaison with local authorities to provide in-service support and training for a wide range of professionals involved in the care and education of young children, and has successfully developed a multidisciplinary degree, the BA in Early Childhood Studies. Her research interests include play and its role in learning and development. At a national level, she was a member of the Council for the Accreditation of Teacher Education (CATE), where she sought to uphold the cause of the early years! She was a member of the Committee of Inquiry into the Quality of the Educational Experience of 3- and 4-years-olds (the Rumbold Committee) and of the RSA Early Learning Enquiry. She acted as consultant to the NFER project 'Early to School – Four Year Olds in Infant Classes'. Her publications include *Play in the Primary Curriculum* with Nigel Hall.
Janet Ackers is a senior lecturer in early years education, at the Manchester Metropolitan University teaching a variety of pre-service and in-service courses. She has had a range of experiences within primary education in general and early years education in particular, including work in a combined nursery centre, nursery

classes and school, as a home–school liaison teacher at a primary school and as an advisory teacher with Manchester LEA's Assessment Development Unit. Her current research interest is assessment and, in particular, the involvement of children and parents in this process.

Janice Adams is a senior lecturer in early years education. She is involved in teacher education courses at both pre-service and in-service levels, including BEd, PGCE and MEd courses. Her teaching experience includes working with young children in a range of settings, including primary schools, nursery schools and classes, and a combined nursery centre. Her recent research has focused on issues of equality of opportunity and on home–school liaison.

Caroline Barratt-Pugh is a senior lecturer in the education studies department and a member of the Early Years team. She has worked in a range of early years settings, particularly with children for whom English is a second language, and in advisory work. Her particular interests include equal opportunities and the acquisition of language. At the time of writing she is seconded to the Department of Language, Arts Education, at the Edith Cowan University, Perth, Western Australia, where she is involved in research and teacher education.

Brenda Griffin is a member of the Early Years team and the multiprofessional co-ordinator in the School of Education. She has developed a variety of in-service courses in response to the Children Act, and has successfully brought together a range of professionals working with young children and their families across the different sectors. She has been involved in the development of the BA in Early Childhood Studies and works extensively with local authorities. Her previous experience has been in the management of combined nursery centres demanding a multiprofessional approach. Her current research interests are centred on young children and their families and ways in which services and the adults within them respond to their needs. Her commitment to the rights of children as defined by the UN Convention is reflected in all her work.

Chris Marsh is a senior lecturer in early years education. She has developed and taught courses for parents, governors and ethnic minority graduates wishing to train for teaching, as well as organizing courses for teachers and other professionals working with young children. Her teaching experience includes working with nursery, infant and junior age ranges involving children from ethnic minority groups and working in special educational contexts. Her major research interests are in nursery education and the relationships between professional educarers and parents which underpin the quality of early years education. She works extensively on local authority in-service courses and acts as consultant to a number of schools and LEAs.

Sylvia Phillips is principal lecturer responsible for teacher education in special educational needs at pre-service and in-service levels. This involves close liaison with schools and local authorities providing support for a range of professionals. Recently she has been particularly involved with teachers, educational psychologists, nursery nurses and special support assistants, helping them to develop in-service courses in the area of emotional and behaviour difficulties across the 0–19 age range. Such projects have resulted in the development of both courses and materials for use by teachers. After some years as a consultant to special schools for children with emotional and behaviour difficulties, she has become increasingly more involved in supporting teachers in mainstream schools in the management of pupils' behaviour.

Rosemary Rodger is a senior lecturer in early years education. She is the research co-ordinator of a joint local authority and university project which is aiming to identify those factors which contribute to quality experiences for children under five. Her previous experiences include organizing in-service training courses for teachers and nursery nurses in the North West of England, and teaching nursery and primary children in several LEAs. She has worked as a home–school link co-ordinator. She has published work on geography for primary school children, evaluation of in-service training for teachers of young children and the place of separate subject knowledge in the curriculum for young children.

Helen Strahan is a senior lecturer in educational studies and has worked in several Manchester inner-city primary schools in both early and later years settings. She was a home–school liaison teacher for four years and continued to pursue her interest in home–school issues through her research and work with both initial training and in-service students. She is course leader for the primary route on the In-service Professional Development Programme and runs courses on home–school liaison, and parental involvement on initial and in-service courses. She is at present engaged in a research project on parental partnership with a local authority.

Acknowledgements

The quality of the educational experience for young children depends upon collaboration at all levels. We are grateful to all those with whom we have been involved for the help they have given us in our attempt to identify quality, for the welcome they have shown us, and for their commitment to young children and their families. In particular we would like to thank Rabina and her family for their contribution and the welcome to their home extended to the author of Chapter 6, and to Lynn Purdon, who as a B. Ed. student became the 'boss' of the builders' yard in Chapter 2.

We are appreciative of the collaboration we have enjoyed with a number of local authorities in the North West of England and the support of colleagues in the School of Education of The Manchester Metropolitan University, in particular Trisha Gladdis for her tireless efforts and unfailing good humour.

Particular thanks are due to the following establishments:
Dorning Street Nursery School, Salford
Dukes Gate Primary School, Salford
Hollywood Park Nursery Centre, Stockport
Mossfield Primary School, Salford
Newall Green Infant School, Manchester
The Dale Primary School, Stockport
Winton Nursery Centre, Salford
and, finally, Salford Education Department for the use of a recording sheet from *Assessment and Record Keeping in the Early Years* (Figure 1.3).

Introduction: The search for quality in the early years

Lesley Abbott

'Quality' is a key word at the present time, with phrases such as *quality assurance, quality control* and *quality time* assuming different meanings depending upon our experience and the context in which we work . The liberal use of the word, however, does not mean that quality is easily defined. For as Harvey and Green (1993: 28) remind us, 'definitions of quality vary and to some extent reflect different perceptions of the individual and society . . . there is no simple definition of quality'. We can all recognize quality in specific situations, but the fact that our views and perceptions are influenced by the context in which we are observing or operating and to a large extent by our mood, feelings and past experiences, means that agreement on a definition of what constitutes quality often remains elusive. For these reasons we have not attempted to define it in this introduction, although some chapters consider quality frameworks and criteria against which provision may be evaluated.

The year 1990 saw the publication of the *Report of the Committee of Inquiry into the Quality of the Educational Experience Offered to 3- and 4-year-olds* (Department of Education and Science 1990), fondly known as 'the Rumbold Report' after the chair of the Committee, Angela Rumbold, who was at that time Minister of State at the Department of Education and Science. The daunting brief with which the Committee was faced included consideration of 'content, continuity and progression in learning, having regard to the requirements of the National Curriculum' and taking account of 'the diversity of needs and types of provision', 'demographic and social factors' and 'the nature of training for teachers and other professional staff involved in the education of children under 5' (DES 1990: 1). All this to be undertaken with an eye to 'the Government's expenditure plans'! One might be forgiven for saying with Hamlet 'ay, there's the rub', for as David (1993: 153) points out:

> instead of comprehensive, multi-functional, affordable provision, the UK muddles on, and instead of investing in its future citizens, helping them early in their lives to learn how to learn, and at the same time ensuring quality of opportunity for women, one is left with the questions: 'How important are young children and their parents in this society, and does this government really want to improve educational standards . . .'

Despite its somewhat pessimistic brief, the Committee sought to identify those issues which contribute to quality experiences for young children and their families. The title chosen for the report by the Committee, *Starting with Quality*, reflects its view that a 'quality start' is the entitlement of every child and the responsibility of every educator.

The degree to which the Rumbold Report has influenced those who commissioned it is unfortunately indiscernible, and the extent to which it has found its way into the establishments in which young children are cared for and educated has depended not only on finance but also on the commitment to quality of those in positions of responsibility. Where it has been used to review provision and practice there is no doubt that it has influenced, in significant ways, the quality of care and education.

For those involved in the training of those adults who play a crucial role in the lives of young children the Rumbold Report has exercised considerable influence. It has not only highlighted important issues to be addressed in the search for quality but also succeeded in bringing together those involved in a variety of services and across different sectors. The move towards multi-professional training and co-ordination of services has accelerated in its wake. *Collaboration, co-ordination* and *quality* are key words at all stages in our lives, as exemplified by Fulgham (1986: 6) when he urges us when we go out into the world to 'hold hands and stick together'.

This maxim is one which, as a group of authors and teachers responsible for the education, training and support of early childhood educators, we as a team hold dear. As the Rumbold Report (DES 1990: 47) points out, 'areas of knowledge and understanding, skills and attitudes will vary', and this certainly holds true for us. We come from a range of backgrounds, disciplines and experiences and have been responsible for the care and education of young children in a wide range of capacities and in numerous establishments. Inevitably, as we seek to share our experiences and concerns and to raise issues for debate, we will present differing perspectives and emphases. We hope that this will provide food for thought and will challenge readers to re-examine their practice and to share their thinking with colleagues. Where we do come together is in our shared belief that young children deserve the very best start in life and that quality experiences are grounded in an understanding of the ways in which young children grow, learn and develop and in a genuine liking for, and commitment to, them and their families.

The various chapters in this book reflect our own areas of interest and experience with young children and with students at various stages in their professional development. Each of us is involved not only with the initial training of teachers on BEd, PGCE, articled teacher and retraining courses, and with the continuing professional development of teachers of young children as they study for higher degrees, but also with multiprofessional training for all those who work with young children in a variety of establishments across the strands of health, care and education.

This book is intended for all those whose lives will touch those of young children and their families. We hope it will be useful to students in training, whether as nursery nurses, teachers, family centre workers, those who are embarking on in-service courses at all levels, parents, managers, governors, advisers and colleagues in further and higher education.

The term 'educarer' is used at various points throughout the book. It is a term coined to describe those adults who provide both care and education, services which cannot be separated when working with young children. As the Rumbold Report (DES 1990: 8) states: 'Care and education for the under-fives are complementary and inseparable.'

We have been much influenced by the publication of the

Rumbold Report, having had 'inside information' from one of our team members who sat on the Committee and has subsequently ensured that we held a copy close to our hearts! This influence can be seen in the format adopted for each chapter, which begins with a quotation from the report which is then exemplified in a case study arising from recent 'shop-floor' experience with young children, their families and educators. In the discussion which follows we are concerned that questions to do with quality are raised; we do not claim to have the answers but in the analyses of the case studies we hope that readers are led to raise questions about their own practice and responsibility for providing quality experiences.

As in the case of young children's learning in which *they* do not compartmentalize, so it has been with us. It has been impossible to avoid overlap and repetition of key issues and beliefs which underpin our work. This repetition only serves to underline those areas of experience which we believe to be central to quality practice and provision.

Having claimed that a precise definition of quality is impossible to achieve because of the nature of young children's learning – as Atkin (1991: 30) states: 'it is messy and unpredictable' – this does not excuse us from attempting to identify those factors which lead to quality experiences. We would claim that quality experiences depend upon key issues, the way in which they are addressed and certain underlying principles being upheld. We turn again to the Rumbold Report (DES 1990: 47), which presents us with a set of summary statements outlining the attributes which adults working in an educational setting should possess in order to provide a high-quality educational experience. These attributes are divided into categories of knowledge and understanding, skills and attitudes; we hope they are reflected in the case studies and discussion presented by each contributor.

Knowledge and understanding
- understanding of the way young children learn;
- understanding the range and importance of play in the education of the young child;
- understanding of the way children acquire language;
- understanding of what is necessary to ensure the provision of *quality* experiences;
- understanding of the varying roles of adults working with

young children and the crucial nature of the role of parents as first educators;
- understanding of factors affecting ease of transition and continuity of experience and ability to employ strategies to avoid discontinuity;
- knowledge of the range of provision, services and contexts in which under fives may be educated;
- knowledge and understanding of the needs and characteristics of young children;
- knowledge of the earlier experiences of children, their home circumstances and any special educational needs;
- curriculum knowledge and understanding of appropriate experience for under fives and ability to relate this to National Curriculum requirements;
- knowledge of recent research and understanding of its implications in relation to the provision of quality experiences for young children.

Skills
- the development of particular skills, interest and expertise in a subject or curriculum area and awareness of appropriate strategies for work with young children;
- skill in planning and implementing the curriculum in order to ensure breadth, balance and continuity with the National Curriculum;
- organisational skills and strategies for effective learning;
- observational skills and effective recording, monitoring and assessment of the curriculum;
- interactive and communication skills – child/child, child/adult;
- management and leadership skills;
- skills in collaborative working, including working with parents and with other professionals;
- skill and ability to provide, or facilitate the provision of, equal opportunity for all under fives notwithstanding differences of race, gender and educational need.

Attitudes
- high expectations of children and self;
- genuine liking for, and sensitivity towards, children and readiness to value them as people in their own right;

- respect for, and appreciation of, the contribution of other adults – parents, colleagues and other professionals;
- a commitment to develop a partnership with parents – with a shared sense of purpose, mutual respect and a willingness to negotiate.

It is no wonder, then, that the Rumbold Committee (DES 1990: 19) conclude that 'working with young children is a demanding and complex task' and that 'those engaged upon it need a range of attributes to assure a high quality experience'.

The chapters which make up this book reflect the range of interests, expertise and experience of a group of people who have worked together over a period of time and are committed to the initial and continuing education of teachers and other professionals involved in the care and education of young children. The School of Education of the Manchester Metropolitan University has forged strong and effective partnerships with schools and a range of other establishments in both public and private sectors. There is a thriving professional development programme which reflects a commitment to multiprofessional development and provides opportunities for all those working with young children in a variety of roles, to come together. This means that students, teachers, nursery nurses, parents, governors, managers and tutors are meeting regularly to share concerns and increase their knowledge, understanding and skills. Some might be embarking on a short course in order to update, refresh or meet an establishment identified need, others might be studying towards a BA or MEd. We believe strongly that knowledge and skills must be shared.

Based as we are within the Faculty of Community Studies, Law and Education, we are mindful of the three recent and major pieces of legislation which in recent years have led to the recognition, by a number of local authorities, that the health, care and education of young children should no longer be the responsibility of separate agencies, but that collaboration among services is essential if quality provision is to be ensured. These are: the Education Reform Act 1988; the Children Act 1989; and the National Health Service and Community Care Act 1990. We are also conscious of our responsibility in providing access to training for all early years professionals and in breaking down some of the barriers which, for too long, have stood in the way of collaboration and openness.

The Rumbold Report provides a strong and central focus for each of our chapters and, along with the Committee of Inquiry:

> We see as essential needs: a closer linkage between the three strands of health, care and education in initial and in-service training; a pattern of vocational training and qualifications for childcare workers which will bridge the gap between vocational and academic qualifications; safeguarding both the rigour and relevance of initial training for teachers of the under fives; and affording improved opportunities of in-service training for childcare workers in educational settings.
>
> (DES 1990: 27)

One of the basic principles of the Children Act 1989 is 'corporate responsibility'. This is defined as the need for social services and education departments to work closely with the health service, voluntary bodies and the private sector in their provision of services to children. Further underpinning of this responsibility comes from the National Health Service and Community Care Act 1989, which expects health authorities, social care and the independent sector to 'respond imaginatively' to the demand for corporate packages of services.

It is our intention that this book will provide something for everyone involved with young children and families. For us, working together is not about taking on more but about letting go of a little, it is about dropping defences, reducing mystique, becoming independent – indeed, about sharing.

We share the Rumbold Committee's view that quality care and education are inseparable, a point endorsed by Brenda Griffin in Chapter 9, where the concept of 'educare' is explored and defined in a discussion of a quality curriculum for the under-threes.

Just as care and education are inextricably linked, so the child and the family must be considered together and partnership between parents and professionals fostered. The Children Act 1989 has been hailed as the most important piece of legislation of the twentieth century as far as the child and the family are concerned. Echoes of the five basic principles put forward in Part Three of the Act can be heard in a number of chapters. The welfare of the child, partnership with parents, the importance of families, the importance of the views of the child and the parent, and corporate responsibility are key elements in establishing firm foundations in the early years. In Chapters 7 and 8 Chris Marsh and Helen Strahan present case studies which point to the importance of establishing 'quality' relationships. Asked for her views on the aims of nursery education, Matthew's mum demonstrates her trust in the nursery staff when she replies:

> *You* learn them what you can't see. I can't go up to you on parents' evening and see it all written up neatly with a tick, but I know it's there. I can see some of the differences in Matthew now but I won't see all of it yet I don't think.

It is clear from her comments that, like the parent in Chapter 8, Matthew's mum 'feels that she belongs'. But what is it that makes her feel like that? We hope that the issues raised in each chapter and the questions posed for consideration by the reader will lead to further thought and discussion, and in the longer term, to quality experiences for staff, children and parents.

In a talk entitled 'By Faith and Daring', in which she celebrated the achievements of women, Glenys Kinnock claimed that 'we [the nation] would never achieve quality unless inequality is dealt with'. In her book of the same name (Kinnock and Millar 1993: 5) she says that 'Government policies must respond to changing patterns of family life and should learn from some of our European partners about social policies which promote equality.' It has been our intention that the issue of equality, in the widest sense of the word, should permeate each of the chapters in this book. Equal opportunity in terms of access to provision, training and education is an aspect of our work to which we are deeply committed. Equality is addressed specifically in Chapter 5 by Janice Adams, in which she presents a rich account of the processes involved in formulating an equal opportunities policy in a nursery centre. Staff, parents, children and the wider community have an equal voice in establishing a way of working which is clearly successful, as evidenced by a parent's assertion (p. 113) that 'she can be whatever she wants to be'. In Chapter 6 Caroline Barratt-Pugh addresses this issue forcibly with regard to the needs of young bilingual children and the responsibilities of educators in responding appropriately and sensitively. For her, early childhood education is a way of collaboratively exploring the relationship between language and learning, language and power, and language and identity.

We need to recognize that the language we use, and the responses we make, reflects the way we value those we are with and the contributions they make. In suggesting ways in which we can help to raise the self-esteem of both adults and children in the primary school, Wetton and Cansell (1993: 27) suggest that 'the words we use in our everyday classroom transactions can easily create positive or negative images and feelings, and although we are becoming increasingly aware of gender and race in terms of classroom language, the common currency of the classroom can often unintentionally belittle children and their contributions'. In Chapter 6 we are urged to 'build on and develop our own understandings of language and individuality'.

Building relationships, raising esteem and developing confidence are recurring themes throughout the chapters which follow. In identifying ways in which children and parents can be involved in the assessment process, Janet Ackers asks in Chapter 3, on behalf of children and parents, 'Why involve me?' and suggests that to involve others can be a powerful tool in helping people to feel good about themselves and in raising self-esteem and motivation. She agrees with Ritchie (1991: 19) that: 'profiling changes relationships within schools, between teachers and children, parents and carers and sometimes between the staff as well'.

This view is echoed by Chris Marsh in Chapter 7, where she claims that 'the relationships between educators and children are recognized as being crucial to the child's emotional security and ability to benefit from the educational environment and the educator's sense of professional development'.

In accepting the Rumbold Committee's definition (DES 1990: 9) of 'curriculum' as comprising 'the concepts, knowledge, understanding, attitudes and skills that a child needs to develop', Rosemary Rodger (Chapter 1) and Lesley Abbott (Chapter 2) consider the ways in which two schools have sought to meet these requirements.

Referring to a number of elements identified by Rumbold (DES 1990: 11) which include careful planning, sensitive and appropriate intervention and an eagerness to learn, Rosemary Rodger presents and discusses a case study of a reception class in which these elements are clearly exemplified. 'This is a *reversible* coat', exclaims four-year-old Kate excitedly, displaying her eagerness to learn and joy in achievement. Sensitive intervention is shown by her teacher as she writes Kate's newly discovered word on the flip chart and involves the rest of the small group of children in discussing their clothing. Words such as 'anorak', 'jacket', 'lining', 'hood', 'zip' and 'mackintosh' fly thick and fast and are responded to enthusiastically by the teacher.

In an examination by the Office for Standards in Education (OFSTED 1993b) of the standards and quality of education in reception classes there was found to be a 'clear connection between good standards overall and the use of a mix of teaching techniques competently including instruction, exposition, demonstration, questioning and listening'. Teachers intervened 'appropriately to sustain and extend activities', they 'used well timed questioning to refine what the pupils were doing and thinking, built on their interests and experiences, explained processes carefully and clarified instructions' (1993b: 9). There is much evidence in the case study in Chapter 1 to support these findings.

However, despite the Rumbold Committee's assertion that play 'has a fundamental role in early childhood education, supplying the foundation upon which learning is built' (DES 1990: 11), when examining the extent to which play was used as a vehicle for learning, the report is less encouraging. It paints a dismal picture of the quality of learning through play, with less than half of teachers fully exploiting the educational value of play. However, where the quality of learning *was* good, as in home corners and water play activities, it was planned into the programme with a sound educational purpose (OFSTED 1993b: 9). Fortunately for those children who are involved in classes where the adults *have* recognized that 'play is a good deal more than recreation' (DES 1990: 11), they are able to engage in 'play that is well planned and pleasurable' and which helps them to think, 'to increase their understanding and to improve their language competence' (DES 1989b: 8).

Such a classroom is visited in Chapter 2, where six-year-old Daniel tells us that 'Play is fun, but it's hard work, too!'. In welcoming his teacher into the building site as the 'boss', he recognized her important role as playmate and endorsed the view held by educationists that adults are far more welcome than they think. There is evidence of sensitive, knowledgeable and informed involvement or intervention on the part of parents, teachers and students which the Rumbold Committee suggests is a prerequisite for quality play.

The children's self-esteem is increased as they take responsibility for assessing their own learning – 'and I thought he was only playing', exclaims Paul's dad.

Effective curriculum planning and implementation is a feature of Chapters 1 and 2. Prerequisites include 'common and clearly-understood aims, objectives and values' and skilled and knowledgeable staff who 'hold high expectations of all children, not limited by stereotyped views about class, cultural background, sex or special educational needs' (DES 1990: 10). In Chapter 4, Sylvia Phillips suggests that in supporting and managing young children with emotional and behavioural difficulties she agrees with the view of the Rumbold Committee (DES 1990: 9) that what is of prime importance is the creation of 'an environment which fosters the development of social relationships and positive attitudes to learning and behaviour'. She presents a case study of a nursery school staff concerned that some children, because of their own or other children's emotional and behavioural difficulties, were not able to profit from the curriculum experiences they were providing. She outlines several key issues for discussion by staff and students, including methods of behaviour management, the need for 'whole-staff' policies and the importance of working in partnership with parents and carers. The case study presented reveals a staff who grew in confidence when they found that planning to manage children's behaviour reduced not only disruption among children but also their own stress levels! She points to the the relationship between high self-esteem and co-operative staff working relationships in the provision of a quality learning environment.

In attempting to define quality in early childhood services, Johansson (1993: 23) states: 'in my opinion quality may be defined in a process oriented way, that is to say via continuous judgment of what happens in specific situations where various factors interplay in a dynamic way'. In an attempt to operationalize quality in early childhood services, she refers to a paper by Lassbo (1993) in which he suggests that:

The degree of quality in the care of young children is represented by the common agreement and satisfaction between

the main care givers, the parents and the child-care person-
nel, on aspects covering the care, the socialisation and the
education of the child.

In Chapter 9, Brenda Griffin points to the fact that very little
research has been done on how children themselves perceive
quality. She points to the work of Katz (1993), who suggests that
educators should put themselves in the shoes of young children
and ask themselves a number of pertinent questions about the
context in which our youngest children are cared for and educated, one of the most important being 'Am I usually glad to be
here, rather than eager to leave?'.

Andersson (1990), in Johannson (1993: 24) describes quality as
an underlying dimension of the daily work in all early childhood
services. He claims that 'quality is what is under the surface, the
persistent daily work done by the staff which can be hard to fully
recognise without being together with a group of children in that
service for a long time'. In a paper presented to a group of early
childhood educators at an international research conference in the
summer of 1993 he suggested that, looked upon in this way, quality
in early childhood services is a question of consciousness. In order
to further this argument he offered the following illustration.

To illustrate what I mean about quality in early childhood
services I will literally move the reader to a shop for oriental
carpets. When such carpets of different qualities are compared they can be judged from various aspects. Here it is a
question of skilled craftsmanship, to know how to tie close
knots, choose good and proper material, but also to have a
good feeling for colouring and an ability to do complex patterns in an artistic way. To make an oriental carpet of high
quality takes, in terms of early childhood service work, a
number of skills which are combined in a way that is mainly
personal and separates the master from the apprentice. When
two oriental carpets, one with high quality and one with low,
are compared it is easy to notice and agree on which one is
the best. But it is much more difficult to explain what conditions caused the differences, it is about a holistic experience
in which the concrete is combined with the sensual. The same
conditions as in this picture from the carpet-shop are significant
for the quality in early childhood services too. It is often easy

to recognise and agree on what good quality is and what is not. But then the difficulties in the analyses begins.

(Andersson 1990)

We are not claiming that analysis is an easy process, but in sharing some of our own descriptions, experiences and analyses of what we have recognized as quality in early childhood care and education, we hope that readers will be helped to analyse their own provision and practice in order that they can claim with confidence, that the children for whom they are responsible are indeed 'starting with quality'.

1

A quality curriculum for the early years: Raising some questions

Rosemary Rodger

> Careful planning and development of the child's experiences, with sensitive and appropriate intervention by the educator, will help nurture an eagerness to learn as well as enabling the child to learn effectively.
>
> (DES 1990: 9)

The above quotation from *The Report of the Committee of Inquiry into the Quality of the Educational Experiences offered to 3- and 4-year-olds* (the Rumbold Report) captures some of the important elements in any discussion about the curriculum for young children. The three strands of the quotation, 'careful planning and development of the child's experience', 'sensitive and appropriate intervention by the educator' and the nurturing of 'an eagerness to learn' are some of the conditions which need to be present for young children to 'learn effectively', and so are essential for an effective curriculum for young children. These three conditions can also be used as criteria for identifying a quality curriculum. Indeed, as the Rumbold Report says, 'good practice owes much to the interplay between the effective planning of the educational activities and the informed judgments of the adults who function as teachers in responding to children's learning' (DES 1990: 38).

It is important to ensure that, however the curriculum is organized, the provision is such that all children experience their basic entitlement to those activities and interactions which will lead them from one stage of their development to the next. What children are able to learn will depend to some extent on what they know already (Bennett 1992). Children use their current ideas to make sense of everyday experiences. This fact is clearly supported by Bruce (1987: 51), who states that in any discussion about curriculum for young children there needs to be consideration of more than the knowledge to be learned. The 'environment is the means of linking the child to that knowledge', and is thus an important aspect. One definition of curriculum which embraces the strands of this chapter is that offered by the Early Years Curriculum Group (1992), which includes:

> all the opportunities for learning at school; all the behaviour that is encouraged or discouraged; the school organization and routines; the way adults, including parents, interact with the children.
>
> (EYCG 1992: 16)

This definition includes those criteria cited in the Rumbold Report quotation at the head of this chapter, but widens it to include consideration of the environment as suggested by Bruce (1987). The processes and structures which a child brings to any situation will also need to be taken into account. I am reminded of a warning given by Alexander (1989) and cited by Anning (1991: 77). In having too broad a definition of curriculum, he says:

> practice becomes talked about less in terms of operational detail than in terms of broad sentiments and commitments; less in terms of learning *processes* than in terms of what is called 'the environment of learning', a kind of conceptual skirting around of the very act which is at the heart of education.

One view may therefore be that the curriculum should aim to encompass what the children know, do and understand in a range of learning areas.

This is the way the curriculum for children under five is described in the *Handbook for the Inspection of Schools* (Office for Standards in Education 1993a: 75). The range of learning areas cited are 'aesthetic and creative; linguistic and literary; math ematical; scientific and technological; physical'.

Discussion about the ways in which these areas support the all-round development of children through their social, emotional, physical and intellectual development would seem to be appropriate and relevant.

However, since the introduction of the National Curriculum in 1989, several curricular definitions for the early years (Manchester City Council Education Department 1992; Sheffield LEA 1992) are beginning to take on the terminology of subjects. There is some support for this in the *Handbook for the Inspection of Schools* (OFSTED 1993a) which offers the following as one of the principles of the education of under-fives: 'to enable children to learn and develop skills, attitudes and understanding which prepares them for continuing education, in particular Key Stage 1 of the National Curriculum'. Although it is clearly recognized in the handbook that the curriculum is not usually taught as lessons labelled by subjects, 'areas of learning or National Curriculum subject headings may be applied to *planning* a high quality curriculum' (OFSTED 1993a: 76). In a recently published report (OFSTED 1993b: 11) many reception class teachers stated that they found the statutory orders and aspects of the non-statutory guidance a valuable backcloth for their work. However, 25 per cent of schools were found to be over-emphasizing sedentary tasks for reception class pupils, with an insufficient amount of time available for exploratory play and a failure to understand the educational potential of play (OFSTED 1993a: p. 9). *The Handbook for the Inspection of Schools* (OFSTED 1993a) very clearly describes the need for children under five to be learning through *enquiry, talking* and *playing*. There are emerging some important questions to be raised in any discussion of a curriculum for the early years.

The case study in this chapter looks closely at the curriculum in action in one reception class where local authority guidelines are used as a basis for the planning of some activities. In this case study they are based upon National Curriculum statements of attainment. Careful planning, sensitive and appropriate intervention, an eagerness to learn, and effective learning will be described and analysed with reference to the case study. Consideration will be given to attention to intended learning outcomes as one way to provide a structure for the teacher, and create the conditions necessary for effective learning. Later in the chapter several early years curriculum guidelines will be reviewed to identify the extent to which statutory curricular requirements for children aged between five and 16 are influencing practice for the under fives. Is this an appropriate way to plan a curriculum for under-fives?

In the past few years there has been much curriculum development activity at local education authority (LEA) level. However, evidence of how newly devised curricular policies for early years children operate in practice is scant and tends to be subsumed within the multitude of surveys emerging from education bodies such as the Department for Education, OFSTED and the National Curriculum Council. The case study which follows describes and analyses a group task undertaken in a reception class in the spring term of 1993. This example was selected because it illustrates how reception class teachers have incorporated an authority-wide policy on assessment and record-keeping into their curricular planning for their pupils. The teacher of the reception class in the case study plans the curriculum around a programme of half-termly topics, which take in all subjects of the National Curriculum (Figure 1.1). The short-term planning of activities is based on the LEA's assessment and record-keeping system and on the knowledge and experience of the reception class team leader who systematically identifies learning objectives for activities which are used to assess children's learning. The planned tasks, children's oral and written contributions and achievement in learning will be analysed using the criteria of quality identified by the Rumbold Report in the quotation at the head of this chapter.

Case study

A group of six children are working with their teacher, discussing the clothes they are each wearing to school that day. The intended learning outcomes have been identified by the teacher in her planning: these focus upon developing the children's oracy, scientific and social skills. It is important to stress that the outcomes are indicators for the teacher to help her structure her interaction with the children and not merely 'can do' checks to be applied to the children. Emma, Hayley, Stuart, Paul, Ashley and Kate are working in the classroom near the coat pegs. Each child puts on his or her own coat from the peg and a discussion follows. 'I've got a coat like that at home' says Emma, as Kate attempts to button up her long raincoat and puts up the hood. Emma stands up to go and get her coat, which is a red and blue checked woollen dufflecoat. Stuart and Paul are weighing all this up and wait to be invited to contribute to the discussion. Emma puts on her coat, and

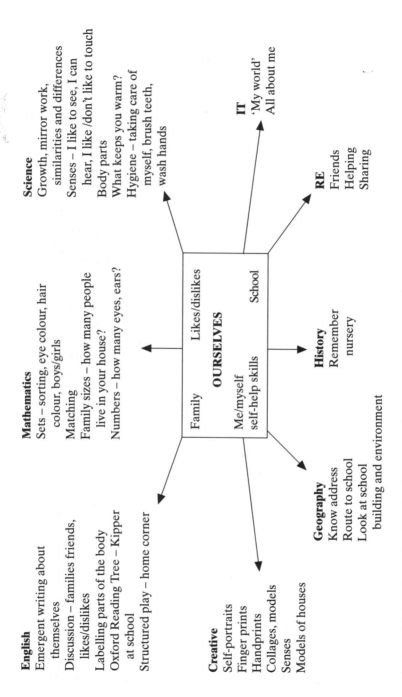

English
Emergent writing about
  themselves
Discussion – families friends,
  likes/dislikes
Labelling parts of the body
Oxford Reading Tree – Kipper
  at school
Structured play – home corner

Mathematics
Sets – sorting, eye colour, hair
  colour, boys/girls
Matching
Family sizes – how many people
  live in your house?
Numbers – how many eyes, ears?

Science
Growth, mirror work,
  similarities and differences
Senses – I like to see, I can
  hear, I like /don't like to touch
Body parts
What keeps you warm?
Hygiene – taking care of
  myself, brush teeth,
  wash hands

IT
'My world'
All about me

OURSELVES
Family   Likes/dislikes
Me/myself
self-help skills   School

RE
Friends
Helping
Sharing

History
Remember
nursery

Geography
Know address
Route to school
Look at school
building and environment

Creative
Self-portraits
Finger prints
Handprints
Collages, models
Senses
Models of houses

Figure 1.1 Half-termly planning in a reception class

the teacher comments on the texture of Emma's coat. 'This feels very soft and furry', she says. Emma shows the lining of the coat, which is artificial fur, saying, 'Look!'. Kate then pulls open her coat exclaiming, 'This is a reversible coat', very proudly. The two girls compare the material from which their respective coats are made. Stuart and Paul continue to look puzzled. The teacher writes 'raincoat' and then 'reversible coat' on the flip chart near by. Stuart and Paul now go and get their coats and put them on. When asked what kind of coat he has got, Stuart answers quickly, 'A jacket'. Paul has an anorak with several badges on it, but he is reluctant to join in with the others as they start to compare what they are wearing with a picture of two children dressed for a very cold day. With gentle encouragement, the teacher invites Paul to name items of clothing worn by the children in the picture and select an item of clothing from an assortment of clothes on a nearby table. She repeats this with the other children in the group and mentally assesses their understanding of which items of clothing are worn on which part of the body, and whether they are able to name different parts of the body. She also assesses their knowledge of colours, which was an unplanned learning outcome for the children as they make a drawing of themselves to go alongside others already mounted on the wall from the same activity carried out with a different group the previous day. Through discussion, 'I have a reversible coat' (Kate) and 'This is my winter coat' (Ashley), a range of classifications are discussed. Duffle-coat, checked coat, jacket, short coat and parka are several examples gathered from the children. The teacher introduces raincoat and encourages the children to describe the raincoat material and the woolly duffle-coat. 'Soft and prickly', says Hayley, describing the duffle-coat. At this point Stuart describes his parka. Further discussion reveals the need to have hoods on coats, wellingtons and umbrellas to keep one dry. This opportunity to observe closely fastenings, zips, buttons and other detail on the coats worn produced drawings at a variety of levels of detail. Some children draw themselves wearing a clearly recognizable coat which they are able to label, while others are drawing barely recognizable figures. These children are in their second term in school.

Throughout the session the degree of collaboration exhibited by the children is high. Confusion with some words is common. A minority of the children are unable to classify the coats in any way. Two children could not yet provide a word for their own coats. However, the children are motivated, enthusiastic about what they are doing and beginning to be able to classify coats according to the material from which they are made. Skilful teacher intervention is used to help Hayley and Paul develop their linguistic understanding.

The teacher is observed on another occasion recalling this activity with about half of the class sitting round in a circle, while the other children are in the library with the nursery nurse. The game being played was called 'My coat is . . .'. One by one the children are describing their coats to each other. 'My coat is red and blue and has buttons', says Kate. 'My coat is long', says Ashley. 'This is my best coat', says Hayley. The teacher prompts the children to add more to their descriptions, using the drawings on the wall to help. She is continually checking the children's responses against her original planning for this activity which clearly outlines the gains in knowledge and understanding which she hopes to achieve. Within her overall weekly planning this is an activity targeted for assessment purposes. An opportunity for reinforcement is provided by the teacher as the children put on their coats at home-time. The accessories are added to the stock of clothes for dressing up in the home corner. The children are observed wrapping themselves up warmly before taking the doll for a walk around the classroom. Ashley and Kate are overheard saying, 'My hands are very warm in these' (sheepskin mittens).

Careful planning

The Rumbold Report clearly expresses the ways in which careful planning can contribute to children's achievements. The Report emphasizes the vital need of the educator to have a sound knowledge and understanding of the various objectives of the curriculum, and how different activities can contribute to their achievement. Planning is seen as the first stage in a continuous cycle (Figure 1.2). It is suggested that we need to organize information in a way which will allow us to:

> pay attention to what is to be learned; understand the relationship between the information being presented and what children already know; understand how children learn; control the rate and quality of learning; and be aware that learning has taken place.
>
> (Ashman and Conway 1993: 49)

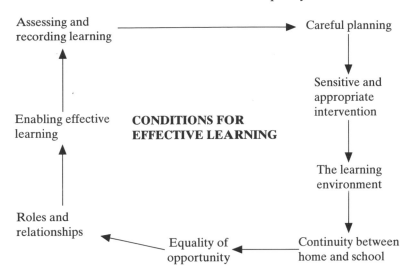

Figure 1.2 The teaching and learning cycle

Thus one can see how planning must be an important dimension in any discussion of a quality curriculum for young children. To suggest that this is an easy task is an over-simplification of the complexities involved. For instance, one very important consideration is the need to ensure that the task matches the abilities of the pupil; extensive knowledge is required on the part of the educator to avoid 'the twin pitfalls of demanding too much and expecting too little' (Central Advisory Council for Education 1967). Traditionally, some early childhood educators (Hurst 1991) and teachers (Brown and Cleave 1991) prefer to allow children to follow their own interests in a child-centred way. Detailed observations of children and records of achievement may be the ways in which progression in their learning and development is recorded. However the curriculum is conceived, there is a need for educators to be clear about their intentions for the children they are educating; this is the message of this chapter. Indeed, curriculum planning and preparation is regarded as one of the key competences of newly qualified teachers (Kyriacou 1991), with successful teachers establishing clear objectives and being able to differentiate children's learning, according to the results of an HMI survey of new teachers in school (DES 1992a).

The teacher in the case study uses the statements of achievement from the LEA assessment and record-keeping system to help her identify learning objectives. As these are based on National Curriculum statements of attainment, she feels she is ensuring continuity with the later years of schooling as well as providing useful guidance for herself concerning the children's potential learning achievement within a range of activities. Cleave and Brown's (1991) research into practice in reception classes between 1988 and 1990 also describes how adults need to know what the child may be learning, although they state that some of their interviewees claimed to provide a multidisciplinary range of activities to enable the young child to develop those skills which may eventually be required for literacy, numeracy, science and so on. The early years teacher in the case study might not subscribe to this view. She is concerned to plan for progression and continuity of learning, and is only able to achieve this through the targeting of specific skills and concepts at the planning stage. Are there other ways of planning in the early years? She wants her team to be able to answer the question, 'What have the children achieved today?'. One dimension not considered here is the children's own view of their achievement, which is described by Janet Ackers in Chapter 3.

The short-term planning identifies a range of learning outcomes based on the statements of achievement in the authority's individual recording sheets (Figure 1.3; Salford Education Department 1990). For example, the teacher plans that the children will meet several learning outcomes from the core subjects. In science it is expected that the children will willingly discuss their observations, name different parts of the body and sort coats to their own criteria. The recording of an object by drawing a picture, the sorting of items for one attribute, the use of a drawing of the coat on a group graph, talking about it and contributing to a group book are planned outcomes in mathematics. Clearly, for children so new to school a crucial outcome is to be seen in terms of an increase in their oracy skills. This is a view upheld by the Rumbold Report, which speaks of 'the importance of talk in children's learning' (DES 1990: 11). Indeed, the recently published survey of practice in reception classes claims that better overall standards of literacy were achieved where the development of spoken English was taken seriously and planned. The teacher plans that the children will be given an opportunity and show a willingness to speak with

SCIENCE RECORD NAME : _____

Can observe and describe what is happening. W.T. A.T. 1	Can describe objects and materials which are hard/soft/bendy/see through. W.T. A.T.3 (Geog W.T. A.T. 3)	Sorts and groups objects to simple given criteria. W.T. A.T. 1 (Ma W.T. A.T. 5)
Sorts and groups objects to own criteria. W.T. A.T. 3 (Ma W.T. A.T.5)	Can differentiate between some colours. W.T. A.T. 4	Can produce sounds in a variety of ways. W.T. A.T. 1 + 4
Can relate simple sounds to their sources. W.T. A.T. 4	Is aware that objects float or sink in water. W.T. A.T. 4	Is aware that magnets can be used to pick up certain materials. W.T. A.T. 4
Realises that heating and cooling can alter the state of certain materials. W.T. A.T. 3	Can predict what might happen. W.T. A.T. 1	
Can name major body parts. W.T. A.T. 2	Notices simple differences between people. W.T. A.T. 2	Is aware of the difference between animals, plants and people. W.T. A.T. 2
Recognises the need to eat and drink. W.T. A.T. 2	Recognises the need for personal hygiene. W.T. A.T. 2	Realises the necessity to dispose of waste responsibly. eg. rubbish in a bin. W.T. A.T. 2
His/her behaviour reflects knowledge of the need for care and safety. W.T. A.T. 1	Is familiar with devices which communicate info. over long distances eg. TV, radio, tel. W.T. A.T. 1	Recognises that a power source may be needed to activate some objects. W.T. A.T. 4
Realises that electricity makes things work. W.T. A.T. 4	Is aware that electricity can be dangerous. W.T. A.T. 4	
Can discriminate between simple weather conditions. W.T. A.T. 4 (Geog W.T. A.T. 1)	Recognises the difference between night and day. W.T. A.T. 4	Recognises that there are different light sources. W.T. A.T. 4
Can identify sun and moon. W.T. A.T. 4		

© Salford Education Department Broughton Road Salford M6 0AQ telephone 061 736 8122

Figure 1.3 Individual recording sheet for science

others; listen to others and interact appropriately; label simple concepts; talk about their own drawing in speech which is audible and capable of being understood by others. For early writing her intentions are that the children will show an interest in what the teacher is writing; believe that he/she can write; write several letters from their own name and differentiate writing from drawing. These outcomes are closely matched to National Curriculum statements of attainment, but as they are for children of non-statutory school age the phrase 'working towards' is used, with reference to National Curriculum ATs on the planning sheets. These act as an observational guide for the teacher, as well as describing indicators of achievement.

Planning for young children needs to be underpinned by the following principle, according to the Rumbold Report (DES 1990: 9): 'how children are encouraged to learn . . . is as important as, and inseparable from, the content – what they learn'. The Report further emphasizes the importance of the context in which learning takes place, as this affects children's responses and the experiences they gain. Nursery guidelines from Sheffield LEA (1992b: 29) are quite explicit in stating that planning needs to identify short- and long-term goals for groups and individuals and, further, that nursery staff must 'take account of the relevant National Curriculum Programmes of Study (PoS) and Non Statutory Guidance (NSG) for core and foundation subjects when planning the curriculum'. The important factor to remember is that not all Statements of Attainment (SoA) are appropriate goals for nursery children (Sylva et al. 1992), which is why the approach adopted by Sheffield which places the emphasis on PoS and NSG is one which might be considered. The question remains as to how far National Curriculum requirements should determine the nursery curriculum.

It is a well-established fact that children will not achieve their intellectual potential in a vacuum which fails to take account of the social context in which the child is learning (Bruner 1975; Vygotsky 1978; Bruce 1987; Schaffer 1992). The intentions of the teacher in the case study clearly take account of the social context by having a series of overall aims for the children's social and emotional development within her planning documents. For example, can the children take turns and share? Do they show respect for other people's work and property? The planning sheet used by the teacher (Figure 1.4) refers to a particular activity,

Activity title _____

Detailed description of what the children are doing

Resources required (how the children are doing the activity)

OUTCOME

Based on statements from figure (1.3) or other learning areas
as appropriate

Figure 1.4   The planning sheet

and the monitoring of this activity in detail provides evidence for assessment purposes.

Sensitive and appropriate intervention

The role of the adult as 'teacher' is of crucial importance if young children are to learn. We have evidence from research (Vygotsky 1978; Sylva *et al.* 1980; Meadows and Cashdan 1988; Athey 1990; Schaffer 1992) to support this. In the context of the above example, the teacher's role as questioner, listener, instructor and demonstrator is important in ensuring that the children progress in their learning. She encourages the children to talk about what they wear to school and, using the knowledge of the other children, is able to support those children not yet possessing the vocabulary for the garment they wear to school. She teaches sensitively, using the picture of children dressed for outdoor play as a stimulus for the children unfamiliar with the range of garments worn to keep warm. It is evident that the some of the children's discoveries about the properties of the materials is clearly new knowledge. Understanding is demonstrated with the help of the teacher, as she encourages the children to wrap up in a selection of accessories: gloves; mittens; hats; scarves; and shawls. The children are prompted to say how they feel wrapped up in this way. Paul, who has grown in confidence, finds wearing a woolly hat and gloves 'very warm', but finds the baseball cap 'fine'. The opportunity to consolidate the knowledge and understanding acquired by the children in a small-group context is provided in the circle game. The teacher builds upon their experiences and enables each child to achieve at their own level of understanding.

Athey (1990: 7) stresses in her research the importance of the teacher: 'although high-quality early learning can take place almost anywhere, it cannot take place without high-quality and appropriate teaching'. The role of the adult as planner, instructor, mediator and explainer fits in with Vygotsky's (1986) theory that children's learning and development should be viewed at two levels (Meadows 1993). The first is that children are able to do some things independently. The case-study children were able to choose from a selection of winter clothes and dress up in the structured play area. They were applying knowledge and understanding gained in another situation to this learning experience.

However, at the second level there are skills and competences which these children need to be taught. This is achieved by the adult asking leading questions, and prompting the children, thus leading the children's learning to a higher level. The coat is red and warm, it will keep me dry if I have a hood and so on. The role of the adult is critical. Bruner (1983) found that adult presence 'strikingly increases the richness and length of play'. Indeed, Wood (1988) suggests that four-year-olds can be taught to do tasks that, alone, they will not master until about seven or eight. 'For them to learn, however, instruction must be geared to that [changing] level of competence. When this condition can be and is achieved, young children can be taught and do learn'. This gap between assisted and unassisted competence is defined by Vygotsky (1978: 86) as:

> The zone of proximal development ... is the distance between the actual developmental level as determined by independent problem-solving and the level of potential development as determined through problem-solving under adult guidance or in collaboration with more capable peers.

Nurturing an eagerness to learn

There are several examples of the children's enthusiasm in the case study. They are motivated and concentrate on the task. This is demonstrated by the way in which they move from one part of the activity to the other. Discussion with the teacher is followed by the ready drawing of their coats and dressing up in a variety of cold weather clothes available in the structured play area. Generally young children's knowledge and interests are stimulated through the chance to engage practically with the activity provided. This will frequently be the result of self-initiation and self-direction (Bruce 1987). The task described in the case study has the following characteristics: the activity is first-hand and within the children's experience; it is based upon experience shared by the children (when it is cold we put on our coat); it is neither self-initiated or self-directed, but very clearly part of a planned series of activities for the reception class children. Does this make it any less appropriate? There is the opportunity for the children to extend the activity into their structured play area and engage in free-flow play (Bruce 1991) to provide the opportunity for self-initiation and self-direction. In the next chapter, Lesley Abbott describes the ways in which children learn through play which is carefully planned and structured by the teacher to provide them with opportunities to develop a range of skills. This is a sharp contrast to the dismal picture of the restricted opportunities for learning through play referred to in the introduction to the report on *Standards and Quality in Reception Classes* (OFSTED 1993b: 9).

There are certains conditions which need to be in place to ensure that children do show an 'eagerness to learn'. The context in which the learning takes place must be considered, through the opportunities 'for children to make sense of the new inputs by constructing links with their prior knowledge' (Bennett 1992). Evidence, too, from Barrett's (1986) research suggests that children need to learn to survive in school and that this process may be more difficult for some children than others because of the mismatch of teacher expectations with children's experiences prior to school or nursery. Willes (1981: 51) reminds us of the range of roles a child takes on when starting school or nursery.

> Children new to classrooms are obliged to learn how to interpret what teachers say, and what constitute appropriate and acceptable responses, and how and when to make individual contributions that teachers recognise as commendable . . . [The child] has to wait his turn, and recognise it when it comes, to compete, to assert his rights, and sometimes to give ground.

Bruner and Haste (1987: 1) highlight the developmental psychologist's viewpoint on the conditions which need to be in place to ensure children are enthusiastic and confident:

> a quiet revolution [has] taken place in . . . the last decade. It is not only that we have begun to think again of the child as a social being – one who plays and talks with others, learns through interactions with parents and teachers – but because we have come once more to appreciate that through social life, the child acquires a framework for integrating experience, and learning how to negotiate meaning in a manner congruent with the requirements of the culture. 'Making sense' is a social process; it is an activity that is always situated within a cultural and historical context.

The children in the case study were secure and confident. They showed great enthusiasm in the activity, evidenced by the way in which it was extended into their 'free-flow' play.

Effective learning

We assume that because the children are motivated, on task and concentrating, we have achieved a situation where the children can learn effectively. But evidence of effective learning is not so easily found. In the education of young children care must be taken to judge effective learning in its widest context and to ensure that in our search for evidence of effective learning we do not fall into the trap of 'missing completely what it is that children are learning because we are so entranced with what we want them to learn' (Drummond 1990). In the previous section I wrote of the shift in the views of developmental psychologists with regard to children as more effective learners in a social context. This has implications for effective learning in classrooms. As Vygotsky (1978) argued: 'Learning awakens a variety of internal developmental processes that are able to operate only when the child is interacting with people in his environment and in co-operation with his peers.' How do we organize the environment to encourage co-operation and concentrated small-group work? Is there a sufficient number of adults available to work with children to extend their learning? Another dimension to a definition of effective learning is the importance of observing children: 'Teachers need to observe children systematically, to structure their learning and to monitor their progress' (Alexander *et al.* 1992: 28). We need also to know that our planning of tasks matches the capabilities of the children. In recent years research carried out by Bennett and Kell (1989: 85) found that among reception class children mismatching was often due to lack of clarity in the teacher's initial instruction to the child. For example, picture sequencing was described as colouring and cutting, and the understanding of shapes was presented as colouring in. They suggested the following sequence of observation and recording of activities in reception classrooms:

1 How is the activity presented?
2 What are the teacher's actual instructions?

3 How clear are they?
4 What is the activity, its supporting materials and adult help?
5 How are children dispersed at points of transitions?

The survey carried out by OFSTED (1993b: 5) is more compli-
mentary of the match of work to children's ability in the reception
class than is generally the case in primary classrooms: 'they were
provided with sound and intellectually challenging teaching related to the first levels of the subjects of the National Curriculum'.
This is in sharp contrast to a survey carried out five years earlier
which said that 'overall, insufficient attention was given to planning an appropriate curriculum for four year olds' (DES 1988: 5).

Reviewing early years curriculum guidelines

The European Commission Childcare Network (Balageur *et al.*
1992: 12) produced a discussion paper to help inform decisions
about quality for young children which includes a list of questions
relating to the learning activities offered to children in a range of
establishments. These are:

Is there a comprehensive range of activities for the children?
Are there opportunities to develop oral and linguistic skills?
Are there opportunities to develop bilingual skills?
Are there opportunities to develop basic mathematical
    concepts?
Are musical expression and musical skills encouraged?
Are artistic skills and aesthetic appreciation encouraged?
Do children have the opportunity to express themselves
    through play and drama, puppetry and mime?
Is interest in biological and scientific concepts encouraged?
Are there opportunities to develop muscular co-ordination
    and bodily control?
Do children understand basic concepts of health and hygiene?
Do children understand about food purchase and food
    preparation?
Do children have an understanding about the local commu-
    nity and the activities which go on in it?
Is the nursery or child care setting equipped with a range of
    furnishings and activities which promote learning?

Can children negotiate some control over the structure and
pace of activities?

This list of questions raises several important issues. Is it appropriate to view the curriculum for young children in terms of subjects?
Can learning be fostered most effectively by conceptualizing
activities in other ways? Do the requirements of statutory schooling exercise a downward pressure on the early years curriculum?
There is a diversity of opinion in the early years field on this very
contentious issue. According to the Rumbold Report (DES 1990),
'educators should guard against pressures which might lead them
to over-concentration on formal teaching and upon the attainment
of a specific set of targets'; nevertheless the curriculum may be
defined and expressed in a number of ways, including 'frameworks
based on subjects, resource areas, broad themes or areas of learning' (DES 1990: 9). The important point to emphasize is not the
way in which the curriculum is described. Planning through subjects may facilitate continuity of assessment and record keeping
with children of statutory school age who are subject to National
Curriculum requirements, and may also enable the under fives
curriculum to dovetail with the primary school curriculum. However, it is the context in which learning activities are presented,
the role of the adult as instructor, and the social and communicative competences of the children which will affect their responses
to the taught curriculum. Consequently, guidance on a curriculum
for the early years needs to embrace all these elements.

Guidance to the Children Act (DH 1991) states that the way in
which experiences are structured affects how learning progresses.
This requires that adults working with young children be skilled
in structuring and supporting that learning, which may sometimes
be planned but at other times inherent in the activities available
for the children: 'With the advent of the National Curriculum,
workers should know in particular which activities enable children
to develop understanding and knowledge of the concepts included
in the curriculum as they approach the age of five' (DH 1991:
152). Thus here also we find mention of statutory curricular requirements in relation to the early years curriculum. Is it too simplistic
to accept this line of thought in helping to define quality criteria
in relation to the early years curriculum because, as is consistently
highlighted, children's responses to activities cannot be isolated to

the domain of that activity only? There are many other factors to be accounted for. In Chapter 7, Chris March considers the importance of the relationships which are formed in the nursery environment; and, in Chapter 8, Helen Strahan considers the context and role of parents in supporting children's learning. Consider the following observations:

> The educator working with under fives must pay careful attention not just to the content of the child's learning but also to the way in which that learning is offered to and experienced by the child, and the role of all those involved in the process . . .
>
> (DES 1990: 9)

and 'all that they see and hear in the environment around them' (Drummond *et al.* 1989: 26). The HMI document on *The Education of Children under Five* (DES 1989b: 8) lists high-quality education as:

1 extending the children's range of profitable learning and experience beyond that which can easily be provided within the family but in ways that are complementary to it;
2 using a range of materials and equipment in planned and progressive ways which stimulates and advances the children's social, emotional, physical and cognitive development;
3 teaching which stimulates and builds upon children's curiosity; enables them to learn through planned worthwhile play activities; encourages them to experiment; to explore their environment; to be imaginative and creative; to plan, implement and reflect upon their experiences;
4 developing children's early knowledge, understanding and skills in ways which provide a sound basis for later education, for example the ability to listen and to talk about and to record their experiences with increasing understanding, competence, confidence and fluency.

These criteria are a broad reflection of the conditions which need to be in place to ensure children have access to experiences of the highest quality, building on activities in the home. The role of the adult in the establishment is described as that of 'teacher', someone who is knowledgeable of the needs of young children and is able to plan and structure experiences which challenge and develop children's learning. This view, emphasizing the centrality of the educator's role, is reinforced in the Select Committee Report (HoC: 1988), which, following visits to USA, noted that where the quality of education was of a high standard, one or more appropriately qualified people were on the staff.

Examination of guidelines for group day care (Cowley 1991: 31) also emphasizes this point. The term 'curriculum' is not used in the guidelines for group day care mentioned above. The term 'activities and equipment for children's play' is how learning experiences are categorized. Further explanation for users of these guidelines elaborates and gives fuller advice as to why it is important for young children to play. The need to plan and organize activities to cater for the wide range of ages in the day nursery is also emphasized. Consideration is given to the wider societal expectations which children will need to meet in their future lives; for example, multicultural education, and equal opportunities according to race and gender are given high status. This is in contrast to the aims outlined in the *Guide to the Children Act* (DH 1991) cited earlier, which state that as a result of the introduction of the National Curriculum workers need to know which activities enable children to develop understanding and knowledge of the concepts included in the curriculum for children over five. Evidence from a survey carried out by Sylva *et al.* (1992) suggests that where social service establishments had examined the requirements of the National Curriculum it was found that there was an increase in communication between under-fives provision and school provision to ensure continuity for the children. There is no evidence in this survey of downward pressure for a more formal curriculum. The area where most change was achieved was in assessment. Many nurseries in the education sector had altered their records to be consistent with the National Curriculum: many records are now placed under the headings which form the structure of the National Curriculum. In describing the changes in her nursery, one experienced teacher in Sylva's *et al.*'s survey said:

We have changed our record cards for children. We used to have a heading called 'block play' where we described what the children built and their language when playing in the block corner ... It's really the same information, only we record it

now under the same headings teachers use in the primary
school – Maths, English.

(Sylva *et al.* 1992: 49)

Are these teachers bowing to pressures from statutory curricular
requirements in moving in this direction?

Another set of curriculum guidelines from the Northern Group
of Advisers (1992) states that the quality of learning and the breadth
and balance of the curriculum in the early years cannot be measured by subject focus alone, since research and effective practice
have demonstrated that young children do not learn in a linear,
compartmentalized or prescriptive way. In order to measure the
quality of learning in the early years educators must:

> monitor the quality of learning experiences which children
> receive (what are the children doing?)
>
> monitor the quality of adult interaction within the learning
> environment (what are the adults doing?)
>
> monitor the quality of the learning environment in which
> learning takes place (what does the learning environment
> look like?)
>
> monitor the quality of plans and policies influencing early
> education practice (how do plans and policies support early
> education?)
>
> (Northern Group of Advisers 1992: ch. 6, p. 3)

These learning experiences can be characterized by children having the opportunity to engage in first-hand experience, solve problem, develop independence and have the chance to interact with
other children and adults. What does emerge from closer examination of these guidelines is the need for greater collaboration
between providers of services for the under-fives to ensure that all
children have the same entitlement to a quality curriculum supported by appropriately trained staff, a point clearly endorsed by
the Rumbold Committee (DES 1990: 27), who

> see as essential needs: a closer linkage between the three
> strands of health, care and education in initial and in-service
> training; a pattern of vocational training and qualifications
> for childcare workers which will bridge the gap between
> vocational and academic qualifications; safeguarding both the
> rigour and relevance of initial training for teachers of the

Table 1.1 Stages in planning the early years curriculum

Stage 1 *What is your starting point?*
What experiences are relevant for the children in your workplace?
What do the children already know?
How do your intentions fit into the institutional planning?
Are you reflecting the institutional philosophy?
This brainstorming may lead to a flow chart of broad ideas.

Stage 2 *You now need to break this down into manageable activities*
How are you going to organise this?
What resources do you need?
Which activities are adult-intensive?
What do you want the children to learn?

Stage 3 To ensure continuity it may be appropriate to make links with the National Curriculum Programmes of Study and Non-statutory Guidance.

Stage 4 *Daily planning and evaluation*
Have you identified learning outcomes in your planning?
Are these relevant for the children?
Which activities might you use for assessment purposes?
What form is your assessment going to take?

Other considerations
How are you going to manage your time?

under fives; and affording improved opportunities for in-service training for childcare workers in educational settings.

In planning, therefore, all educators, including students and newly qualified teachers, may find the stages presented in Table 1.1 appropriate to go through. This staged process was devised in collaboration with a group of Liverpool nursery and reception class teachers on an in-service course.

Examination of national policy statements and local authority guidelines does in some cases have conflicting messages for practitioners. It is important that a statement based on a consensus viewpoint is agreed by workers in the early childhood field to ensure all children, whatever their route through child care in the early years, are receiving an experience which is commensurate with their age and stage of development and which recognizes and values the research which has been carried out in the past ten years into the 'immense cognitive competence' of our children under five (Alexander *et al.* 1992). A curriculum, however it is described, must allow all children to have access to skilled professionals, an environment which supports early learning and resources which support professional workers in their aim to provide equality of educational opportunity for all children. The principles which underpin this curriculum must be clearly articulated to all involved, both parents and educators, to ensure a shared understanding is developed and children become 'effective learners'.

Issues for discussion

1 Discuss the advantages and disadvantages of using National Curriculum Programmes of Study as learning objectives in your planning.
2 We would all accept the importance of talk in children's learning. How do you ensure provision for quality talk in your establishment?
3 Young children learn most successfully when they are keen and eager. Using your own observations, discuss the characteristics of keen and eager learners and the contexts in which you observe this.
4 How do you know your children are 'effective learners'?

Suggested further reading

Aubrey, C. (ed.) (1993) *The Role of Subject Knowledge in the Early Years of Schooling*. London: Falmer Press.
Dowling, M. (1992) *Education – 3 to 5*. London: Paul Chapman.
The Early Years Curriculum Group (1989) *The Early Years Curriculum and the National Curriculum*. Stoke: Trentham.

2

'Play is fun, but it's hard work, too!' The search for quality play in the early years

Lesley Abbott

> Play that is well planned and pleasurable helps children to think, to increase their understanding and to improve their language competence. It allows children to be creative, to explore and investigate materials, to experiment and to draw and test their conclusions . . . Such experience is important in catching and sustaining children's interests and motivating their learning as individuals and in co-operation with others.
>
> (DES 1989b, cited in DES 1990: 11)

Approaching Milton Keynes on a recent train journey to London, I happened to look up from the inevitable marking which accompanies me on any trip, to read on a large hoarding the words 'Work easy – play hard' (in smaller letters underneath it was the message 'Word-processing made easy with Microsoft').

The previous day I had been working with a group of year 1 children and a student in the structured play area which had been established in their classroom. I had also been involved in a study of the perceptions of play held by staff, parents and the children themselves, and on seeing this advertisement the words of Daniel, aged 6, with whom I had been talking the previous day, sprang to mind: 'Well,' he said thoughtfully, 'play *is* fun, but it's hard work, too!' These words provide the focus for this chapter. Fun *is* what we all recall about our own play experiences, but in many cases play involves much more, and for play to be successful and enjoyable it often involves hard work.

At any one time in play children can be required to collaborate, negotiate, make choices, organize, explain, lead, communicate, share, take responsibility, ask and answer questions, record, interpret, predict, recall and reflect. No wonder, then, that Daniel considered play to be hard work! In the case study which follows, in which Daniel played a leading role, I would maintain that a range of quality experiences were gained by both children and adults. Defining quality, particularly in an area like play which itself seems to defy definition, presents us with problems and calls to mind the words of Bruner (1980), who wrote of play as 'something which everyone recognises but no one can frame . . . into a single impeccable definition' – and so with quality!

However, we would be shirking in our duties as professionals if we made no attempt at all to pinpoint what it is about an activity or experience which makes us say we must have more of it. In that vein, therefore, when considering what is meant by 'quality' in play and what we should look for when attempting to identify those factors which contribute to a rich and meaningful experience for children and adults, a number of important points spring to mind.

The first is to do with 'ownership' and the degree to which children are involved, not only in 'playing', but in any decisions about the focus and planning of the activity. How often do adults and children talk about play? The second concerns the purpose and the degree to which views are shared and children understand the purpose of the activity. Third, quality play often depends upon quality resources and involvement on the part of the adults, yet research reveals both a lack of quality materials and play environments and a reluctance on the part of adults to become involved in play. The valuing and sharing of children's play by adults can only serve to increase the status of the activity and the self-esteem of the child. Finally, play must be capable of meeting curriculum requirements and of facilitating learning in a number of areas, including both cognitive and affective domains. It should provide for equality in terms of access and opportunity for all children, regardless of gender, race and special educational needs.

In answer to the question 'what are children learning through their play?', Atkin (1991: 11) suggests that we turn the question on its head and consider what they are not learning.

In play children are not learning to fail, to seek right answers, to accept what adults tell them without question, to parrot rote responses, to stop doing something because they can't get it right, to become a spectator to others rather than a participant in whatever field of interest.

In examining the following case study of children at play, it is important to consider how far it is possible to identify some of these characteristics and factors which affect the quality of children's experiences in play.

Case study

'Welcome To The Dale Construction Site' declares the notice in the corner of the busy year 1 classroom in The Dale Primary School. Emma and Paul are 'on site' selecting, from a wide range on offer, the tools they will use to construct the building being designed by Daniel and Sarah at the drawing board in the office next door. A notice announcing that 'This is a hard hat area' reminds the builders of the importance of safety, and Paul takes a brightly coloured builder's hat from the appropriately labelled hook and places it on his head before he begins to study the plans.

In the drawing office the children discuss the client's requirements – consulting previously drawn-up plans, appropriately stored in plan chests, to help them decide where they should place the main entrance. Sarah pauses to answer the telephone – it is the 'boss' of the site, in the guise of the teacher phoning to ask for additional supplies of roofing tiles to be delivered to the site as soon as possible. The message, time received, quantity required and action taken, are recorded on the pad lying in readiness by the phone. In a voice which suggests that she has been at the job all her life Sarah deals with the request, adding 'Yes, I know – but we are working as quickly as possible and we will try to deliver on time'. Meanwhile 'on site' Emma and Paul discuss the relative strengths of the tile cement, reading accurately from the various tubs among which they must make a choice, and where a particular word eludes them, making an intelligent guess, applying the skills they have acquired in the more 'formal' aspects of their language work.

The 'builders' are supported by an environment full of information and displays which reflect exciting first-hand experiences

covering a range of subject areas. Visits have been made to builders' yards, conversations have taken place, new vocabulary has
been acquired, names of materials and 'builders' have been learned,
as evidenced by Daniel's insistence on his change of name to Bob,
'cos it's more "suitable" for a builder'! Experiments have taken
place in order to test the strength and suitability for the job of
a variety of materials, and the results have been carefully and
appropriately recorded.

Environmental walks provided opportunities for increased
observational skills and knowledge of the variety of housing and
other buildings in the area. Photographs taken by the 'builders'
themselves, and others loaned by local estate agents, only too
willing to be involved, have widened their knowledge, vocabulary,
skills of perception, discrimination and communication, and above
all increased motivation and confidence in being able to see the
relevance of these various experiences.

Once the houses, carefully planned and designed in the drawing
office, have been built on the adjoining site, 'For Sale' notices go
up and adverts are drafted and redrafted in order to get the wording just right in order to attract 'first-time buyers'.

The children adopt a variety of roles as interested potential
buyers come along to view the property, appropriately dressed
and with mannerisms and accents carefully discussed and adopted.
The language of negotiation, of buying and selling, vocabulary
which includes words like 'conveyancing', 'contracts', 'surveyor'
and 'mortgage' are used and the role of the building society is
introduced.

Parents are involved in school and in the various fact-finding
visits and excursions which take place. This type of involvement
provides opportunities for discussion with staff and children and
for observation at first hand of the potential for learning of this
type of activity within the early years curriculum.

But the questions remain: What are the children learning, and
how do we know? What is the purpose of this kind of activity
which, if it is to be a 'quality experience', must be well planned
and carefully thought out? It is important that teachers are able to
justify the approach and for parents and children to see the meaning and relevance of what they are engaged in.

Let us examine this case study, of what I would call a 'quality'
play experience, in the light of the claims made about play by

HMI (DES 1989b) at the beginning of this chapter and endorsed by the Rumbold Committee. The first claim is that 'Play that is well planned and pleasurable helps children to think, to increase their understanding and to improve their language competence'. There is no doubt that the play was well planned by both staff and children. National Curriculum requirements had been carefully considered and incorporated into an experience which was carefully discussed, was relevant, purposeful and of which the children had a sense of ownership. An examination of the variety of houses to be found in their area and a visit to the local builder's yard served to increase the children's geographical awareness in line with the programme of study for Geography at Key Stage 1.

> Much of pupils learning at Key Stage 1 should be based on direct experience, practical activities and exploration of the local area.
>
> (DES 1991: 31)

The detailed planning documents kept by the teacher ensured that curriculum balance was achieved and opportunities were provided for children to practice the skills they had acquired in the more 'formal' aspects of their lives. Witness Paul's experimentation with 'apostrophe s' as he lists the materials required in the builders' yard (Figure 2.1).

He had been taught a rule by his father and confidently applies it in his play. When questioned about the apostrophe he replied: 'Whenever you see an "s" at the end of a word you add that little squiggle!' We may question the wisdom of the teaching, but there is no doubting the fact that the play situation gave him the confidence to experiment and try out his newly learned skills, as in his use of phonetic spellings such as 'sment', something he might not have done in a more formal, teacher-directed activity labelled 'English' on the timetable.

There is also much evidence, not only from talking with and playing alongside the children in this sequence, that the play was pleasurable, but also from studies of children's perceptions of the activity. In a study of Swedish pre-school children, Karby (1989) found that they were able to differentiate play from other activities that are often called 'play' by adults. While enjoyment and pleasure are high on the list when they are asked for their views about play, it is also clear that children regard their play as highly

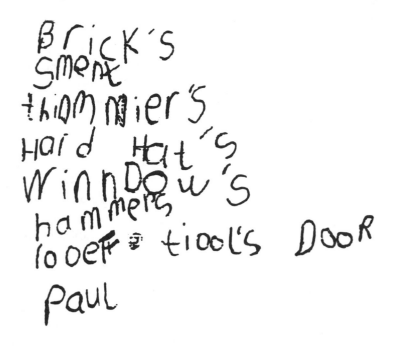

Figure 2.1 Paul's list of materials for the builders' yard

significant and important. 'Play *is* hard work, but it is also fun', said Daniel, one of the builders, as he chewed his pencil while deciding on the materials he needed to build the new house. Talking to children between the ages of three and seven about play, the recurring theme appears to be the relationship between freedom and fun and the opportunities for learning. 'You can write whatever you like in this big book', said Natalie as she sat at the desk in the 'office'. 'I know, look at this, it tells you the days of the week and the months and the year!' replied her friend as she discovered the wall calendar. Talking with the children revealed their pleasure in exploration and discovery and their joy in sharing their newly found knowledge with sympathetic adults in a non-threatening environment.

There is ample evidence in the play sequence described that children are thinking hard about what they are doing. Emma and Paul, in having to decide which tub of tile cement to use,

are 'reading' both written and pictorial clues and justifying their
decisions using new vocabulary and language forms in appropriate
ways.

They are fascinated by the new words which they encounter –
listed in the 'office' and reinforced by the adults who play with
them as they 'work' hard to understand the meanings. There is
ample evidence that, in year 1, they are still enjoying playing with
words – something we associate with younger children (Opie and
Opie 1959). An example of this playing with language occurred
when Sarah was introduced to the word 'inventory' as she took
stock of the materials. As she wrote she could be heard singing
to herself 'inventory, story, gory', but the difference between
the three-year-old and the six-year-old was apparent when she
revealed her understanding of the word as she explained to Paul
what she was doing: 'I'm writing what we've got and how many so
I'll know what to order – this is how it has to be done in this big
book' (Figure 2.2). Increasing language competence is a major
goal for all those engaged in the education of young children and,
as we are informed by National Curriculum Council (1990) documentation: 'In role play areas children can practice recently learned
and emerging skills'.

It is not only competence in using language which is apparent
in these examples but also the negotiation and construction of
shared meanings. Language does not occur in a vacuum; studies
such as those by Tizard and Hughes (1984), Wells (1985) and Hall
(1987) point to the importance of purposeful language occurring
in a natural context in which adults facilitate and value children's
language learning by responding to them as appropriate language
users – a point discussed with reference to young second language
learners in Chapter 6.

It is clear that this was happening in the play of these five- and
six-year-olds. It was also apparent that they were being creative,
not only in their use of language, but also in the roles they adopted
and in the imaginative ways in which they were using the resources.
The second part of the quotation with which this chapter begins
is worth examining in this respect: 'It allows children to be creative, to explore and investigate materials, to experiment and to
draw and test their conclusions'.

The building site had been planned to provide the children with
opportunities to make sense of what was happening in their imme-

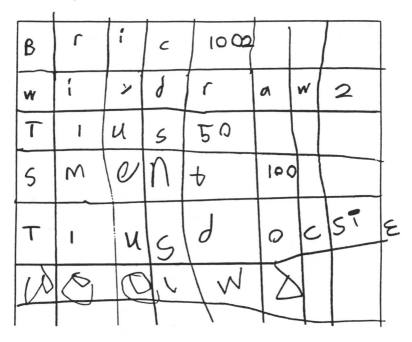

Figure 2.2 Sarah's inventory

. diate environment as a new housing estate was being built, and to meet National Curriculum requirements in science, maths and English. In reality it achieved far more than this; Atkin (1991: 34) observes that while

> good quality play is not a necessary condition for better achievement on traditional measures of performance, that is I.Q. tests and reading and maths tests, it does foster other competences that may be equally, if not more important, for example self-esteem, task orientation, attitudes to learning, persistence, flexibility and creativity.

There is no doubt that in the experiments which the children were required to conduct in testing the strength and suitability of a range of building materials and in recording their results they learned a great deal and met the required attainment targets. It is

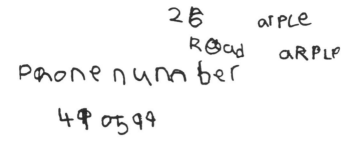

Figure 2.3 Lisa's letter of confirmation

also evident that in solving the problems with which they were faced they became persistent and task-orientated, in accommodating the needs and wishes of others they learned to be flexible and creative, and as they experienced success their self-esteem increased by leaps and bounds.

The confidence with which Lisa, unaided, wrote to confirm that Emma could become a builder as long as she conforms to the rules they have made as a group is apparent in her letter (Figure 2.3) and was certainly evident in her play.

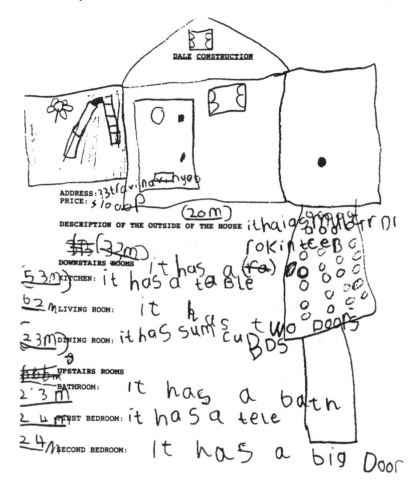

Figure 2.4 The information sheet produced by Paul and Daniel

Following their visit to an estate agent and their subsequent discussion of the literature provided, Paul and Daniel collaborated in producing an information sheet about the house which they had designed and built (Figure 2.4). They included a picture, address, price, room measurements and imaginative descriptions as to the room's contents.

An important factor influencing the quality of the children's learning and achievements is the trust placed in them by the adults with whom they worked. In examining some of the possible limits on creativity in play (Bruner 1980: 79) points to the 'control' exercised by parents, friends, and teachers as placing limits on and in some cases blocking the child's capacity to be creative. In this case study the support rather than control offered to the 'builders' to explore and experiment with new skills without fear of failure or recrimination was instrumental in the success of the activity and is endorsed by the Rumbold Committee (DES 1990: 11) when they agree with HMI that: 'Such experience is important in catching and sustaining children's interests and motivating their learning as individuals and in co-operation with others.' They suggest that a key element in the search for quality in the play of young children is the adult – in particular, adults to whom they have easy access and who will 'stimulate and encourage dialogue ... adults who offer views, ideas and observations and who "think aloud" elicit children's thoughtful participation more effectively than those who control the conversation, or those who do not intervene'.

Bruce (1991: 17) makes the claim that: 'Playing together gives children the opportunity to use language in an active, functional and comprehensive setting.' Evidence of this can be seen in Emma's letter (Figure 2.5) informing the builders that an inspector is on his way. By adopting the role of potential house buyer the teacher was providing these opportunities as well as signalling that it was legitimate and acceptable for adults to play with children.

Bruner (1980) refers to the fact that adults are far more welcome than they think in children's play, yet there is a reluctance on their part to become involved. Indeed, this reluctance has increased and in the face of external pressure may not be based so much on the adult feeling either inadequate to the task or fearing that involvement might spoil or disrupt children's play, as on the feeling that in the present climate there is no time to play and that it is not part of the teacher's role. Tyler (1990: 10) refers to the

high levels of anxicty which continue to be generated by teachers charged with putting the National Curriculum into practice. Under the strain of what they may perceive as the many conflicting demands being made on them some teachers may yield to a temptation to adopt a more formal approach as a coping strategy.

Figure 2.5 Emma's letter to the builders

It was heartening to discover that in this particular classroom play was seen as a high-status activity and acknowledged by staff, parents and children as a legitimate area in which all of them could be involved. It was also clear that careful thought had been given to ways in which the requirements of the National Curriculum would be met, how assessment would take place, where play featured in the development plan, and the school's commitment to continuity, progression in learning and the endeavour to provide a broad and balanced experience for the children.

In order to provide successfully for play of this quality, the staff have to be both confident in what they are doing for children and able to justify the attention it is afforded within the school. Parents must also be convinced of its value, and one of the best ways of doing this is to involve them in the activity. In both designing and selling the houses, once built, the parents became fully involved. In a study of parents' views about play (Abbott 1993) the predominant response from parents of children aged from three to seven was 'I didn't realise just how much children learnt through play'. The amazement of a father on being told by his six-year-old son that on visiting a building site with him at the weekend he was 'contravening the safety rules!', by not wearing a hard hat, had to be witnessed to be believed. 'He knew what it meant too – that's what baffles me – he wouldn't have come across that word normally at six would he?' was the parent's response; 'and I thought he was only playing!'

Despite the vast amount of research on and the contribution of many eminent educationalists to our understanding of the importance of play in early learning, teachers are constantly having to justify – not only to parents but also to politicians and, sadly, to colleagues at other stages within the profession – children's play as worthwhile and not simply a pleasurable occupation or something to be done when 'work' is completed.

Atkin (1991: 30) suggests that adults are afraid of the messiness and unpredictability of play, in which neither the player nor the content are under their control. They distrust the irrationality of some kinds of play, the fact that it is not directly utilitarian and that assessing its outcomes is not easy.

This latter point is particularly important in the present climate when assessment has taken on new meanings and for some people is equated only with testing. Under the Education Reform Act 1988 assessment has become a statutory process, combining continuous teacher assessment with the results of Standard Assessment Tasks (SATs) in maths, English and science. It is important that early years educators continue to carry out their own informal and non-statutory assessments, because, as Drummond and Nutbrown (1992: 23) point out:

The statutory requirements for the assessment of seven year olds, laid down in the Education Reform Act 1988, represent only a part of the whole process of assessment. There is much more to know about young children than their levels of attainment in Maths, English and Science at the end of Key Stage 1.

Close observation of, and interaction with, children in play will tell educators a great deal about their needs and development. Bruce (1987: 25) identifies a number of key principles which should underpin early childhood practice. She claims that: 'What children *can* do, rather than what they *cannot* do, is the starting point in the child's education'; 'and so,' as Drummond and Nutbrown (1992: 93) point out, 'by implication it is the starting point of assessment too'.

In drawing his plan for the house he was going to build, Daniel was able to show his teacher just how far his spatial awareness had developed, as well as his level of understanding of the task, hand–eye co-ordination, skills in using language, and social skills as he co-operated, negotiated and took on a leadership role. The diagnostic value of play cannot be over-emphasized; close observation of children in play guards against unrealistic expectations being placed upon them. Interaction with children in play that is well planned and purposeful allows staff to monitor not only the children's progress but also their own success in achieving the goals they have set. Careful recording provides evidence of progression and development in a whole range of areas which neither more formal methods nor simple checklists will pick up. The issue of assessment is dealt with in much more detail in Chapter 3, where the child's own involvement in self-assessment is explored. It is significant that on the building site children were much more open and honest in acknowledging what they could and could not do, and in recognizing and advertising the skills and achievements of others, than they were in other more formal learning situations.

In terms of equal opportunities, the building site proved an ideal vechicle through which stereotypical roles could be challenged, not only in role play, as boys and girls equally happily adopted the roles of office worker, 'boss' of the site and builders, but also in the discussion which took place afterwards, as pictures and stories of men and women in a variety of roles were examined. The importance of providing equal opportunties is investigated in some depth in Chapter 5 and Chapter 6, as is that of the child with special educational needs in Chapter 4. What is significant in both these respects is the child with limited spoken language and social skills who, having been encouraged to play in this area and finding her views valued, was able to express herself clearly and with some force. When asked by the teacher, who had adopted the role of 'boss' of the building site, whether it was all right for a woman to be in charge, she replied 'Of course it is as long as she can shout at them!'. Why did this happen? I suggest that because children felt 'comfortable' in the play situation, and they saw that their views were accepted and valued by the adults who were in there playing with them, they were able to take risks, to try out new roles and to express themselves clearly and honestly without fear of reprimand or failure. As Purdon (1993: 43) concludes in her study of play and early writing, 'by taking risks children develop signs of autonomy and hence independent learning' and 'independent learners are intrinsically motivated learners. Surely our ultimate aim?' Having observed her teacher adopt what has been traditionally accepted as a male role, that of 'boss' of the building site, Emma happily donned the hard hat and became quite assertive and dominant in her dealings with the other builders. By sharing the play, modelling alternative roles and styles of communication, adults can do much to build children's confidence and self-esteem and to raise the status of play in the eyes of the players.

Difficulties encountered in attempting to define both 'play' and 'quality' are due to the fact that they are largely context-dependent. In our quest for 'quality' we are helped by the Rumbold Report (DES 1990: 11) to recognize that:

Play underlies a great deal of young children's learning. For its potential value to be realised a number of conditions need to be fulfilled:

(a) sensitive, knowledgeable and informed adult involvement and intervention;
(b) careful planning and organisation of play settings in order to provide for and extend leaning;
(c) enough time for children to develop their play;
(d) careful observation of children's activities to facilitate assessment and planning for progression and continuity.

For all of us involved in the care and education of young children the conclusion reached by the Rumbold Committee must be central to our work:

> We believe that it is vital for all adults with responsibilities for young children to recognise that, for them, play is a good deal more than recreation. It has a fundamental role in early childhood education, supplying the foundation upon which learning is built.

(DES 1990: 11)

Having eavesdropped on a group of children engrossed in and clearly enjoying their play, we may not be much further on in our quest to find an impeccable definition of either 'play' or 'quality'. What is clear is that the activity *was* purposeful and enjoyable, and that many of the processes identified as important within the framework and requirements of the National Curriculum were evident in this particular play activity. These include:

- collaborating;
- making choices;
- organizing;
- explaining;
- talking and communicating;
- sharing;
- taking responsibility;
- asking and answering;
- recording;
- interpreting, predicting, recalling and reflecting.

Those who claim that play and the National Curriculum are uneasy bedfellows are urged to think again.

Further practical activities

1 Try to identify the skills concepts and processes involved within a play activity in your own classroom or learning environment.
2 Individually, or as a staff, try to answer the following questions:
   (a) What opportunities do you provide within your establishment/classroom for children to engage in the processes listed at the end of the previous section?

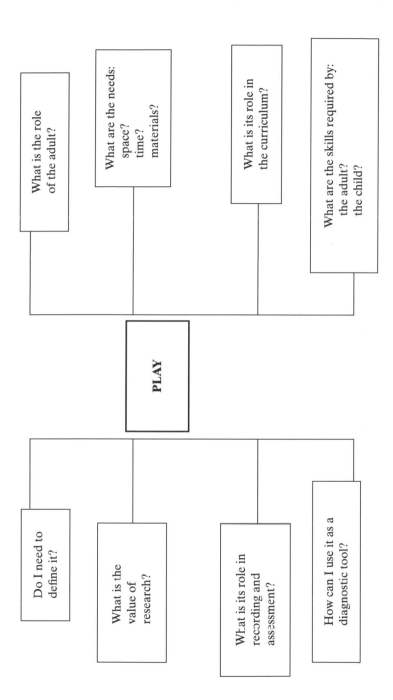

Figure 2.6 What do I need to ask about play?

(b) What role is played by the adult?
(c) In what ways do you consider that the play activities within your establishment/classroom provide for equality of opportunity for children and adults?
(d) Identify the ways in which play provides opportunities for assessment by adults and children.
3 Consider each box in Figure 2.6 and relate it to the play provision made in your establishment/classroom.

Suggestions for further reading

Bruce, T. (1991) *A Time to Play*. London: Hodder & Stoughton.
Hall, N. and Abbott, L. (1991) *Play in the Primary Curriculum*. London: Hodder & Stoughton.
Moyles, J.R. (1989) *Just Playing? The Role and Status of Play in Early Childhood Education*. Milton Keynes: Open University Press.
Moyles, J.R. (1994) *The Excellence of Play*. Buckingham: Open University Press.
Northern Group of Advisers (1992) *Right from the Beginning*. Publications Unit, Gateshead Metropolitan Borough Council, Education Department.

3

'Why involve me?' Encouraging children and their parents to participate in the assessment process

Janet Ackers

> Careful assessment and record-keeping underpin all good
> educational practice. They are essential elements in securing
> effective continuity and progression . . .
>
> (DES 1990: 16)

'I done that, it mine', exclaimed three-year-old Peter excitedly, sharing his profile with me at the 'Stepping Stones' pre-school group. 'Jane put that in cos it's nice, there's all different colours in it', Melissa, a nursery child, informed me while proudly talking me through the photographs, paintings and drawings in her profile, or, as she called it, her 'book'. 'I want to choose these 'cos they're the best', Robert told the reception class teacher, who was sitting with a group of six children helping them to select work from their drawers and books to put into their profile folders. Asked by her teacher why she had chosen a particular piece of work for her profile folder, Paula replied, 'Because it's nice, the colouring's neat and I've done the drawing nice'. 'I like this work because it is colourful and it is neat and I think my mum will like it. I don't know if my teacher likes it but I know I do. It has a nice border, it has nice colouring', wrote Sally on a proforma to accompany her profile selection (Figure 3.1). David, a boy in the same year 2 class, wrote, 'I like this work because I tried hard'.

These comments are typical of those made by children in the infant school where I carried out research into self-assessment. Children are involved in their own assessment from a very early age as part of a whole-school approach to profiling, in which parents also play a leading role. At the school, children and parents are seen as important contributors to the assessment process.

Why involve children and parents in assessment? What role can they play in assessment and record-keeping? Will their involvement lead to effective continuity and progress, in terms of children's learning and the process of assessment? Does the profiling approach add to the quality of assessment for young children? This chapter aims to explore these questions with reference to one school's approach to profiling.

Profiling is not a new idea. According to Ritchie (1991), it had its origins in the Newsom Report, *Half our Future*, (Central Advisory Council for Education 1963). The roots of the movement lie in secondary education, where some teachers have been working with profiles and records of achievement since as far back as the early 1970s. More recently, the interest in profiling has moved into primary education, as Murphy (1991: 145) states: 'Many primary schools have already been influenced by the move towards profile reporting in secondary schools and DES circulars heralding a national move towards producing records of achievement for all school pupils.' Although the promise of a national system of records of achievement, in place by 1990, has now been withdrawn, this method of assessment has been put forward by the Schools Examination and Assessment Council (1991) as a form of ongoing record for primary schools. However, the importance of profiling and records of achievement seems to have waned, with the effort going into developing the National Curriculum and its testing programme. Or is it, as Kelly (1992: 15) claims, 'because its conceptual base clashes with that of that programme'? In spite of this, many schools are still holding on to the concept of profiling and trying to marry this approach with the National Curriculum and its assessment requirements. Why? Perhaps it is because 'profiling changes relationships within schools, between teachers and children and parents/carers and sometimes between the staff as well' (Ritchie 1991: 19), and because 'they have tended to become a dynamic influence on the whole teaching and learning process' (Murphy 1991: 145).

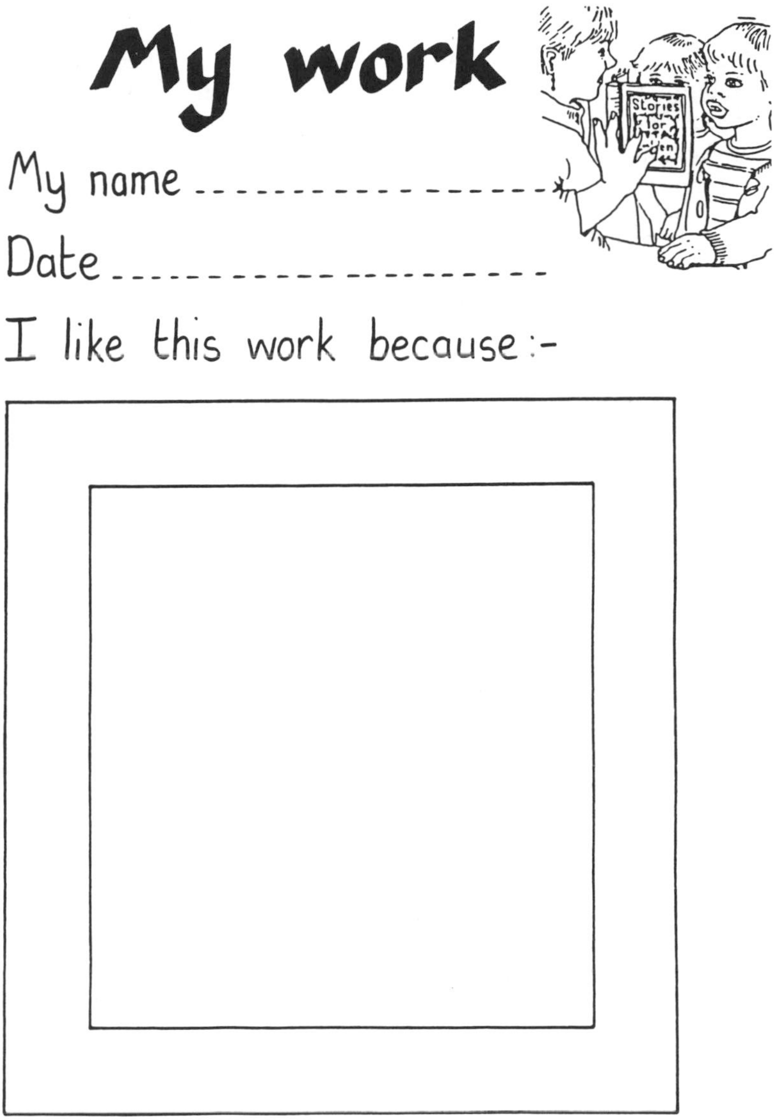

My work

My name -

Date -

I like this work because :-

Figure 3.1 Proforma used to accompany work selected for the profile

What is profiling? It can be defined as:

> The overall formative process of assessing, recording and gathering evidence of progress and achievement. This process should involve the child, teacher and parent(s) in order to provide a basis for decision-making about the next stage of learning for the child.
>
> (Manchester City Council Education Department 1990)

The record which is developed through the profiling process is often referred to as a 'profile'. This can be described as a 'composite of information collected to form an album of a child's achievements, in and out of school' (Manchester City Council Education Department 1990).

It is essential that the profile positively reflects the child's achievements. What should go into the profile? Manchester City Council Education Department (1990) suggest that the following items could be included:

- samples of the child's work;
- narrative comments on the child's personal development;
- diagnostic information;
- details of learning styles;
- personal factual details;
- personal achievements outside the school/school day.

There is no set format for profiles. The school previously mentioned uses A4 ring binders and A4 vinyl wallet type folders (the latter provided by the local education authority) in which to store the information. I have also seen 'home-made' profiles in book form made from large sheets of sugar paper sewn or stapled together, with the information glued on to its pages. However, the format is a matter of personal choice and there are many variations. It is the underlying principles of the profiling process that are the important issue.

Profiling tends to be more pupil-centred than other methods of assessment, with self-assessment a major feature. Research, mainly in secondary schools, has provided evidence that pupils become more involved in and reflective about their work if they are involved in assessment and this in turn benefits their learning. Indeed, as Lally and Hurst (1992: 73) comment, involving children in their own assessment 'is consistent with the growing view that children should be encouraged to develop as autonomous learners with a valid viewpoint'. Is this what is happening to Sally, one of the children cited above, who stated: 'I don't know if my teacher likes it but I know I do'?

Another important element of profiling is the involvement of parents or carers in the assessment process, not only in receiving or sharing information about their children but also in contributing towards the recording of their achievements. Ritchie (1991: 108) believes that:

> Parents and carers have a crucial role to play in the profiling process. Parental support and participation is thus seen as being essential for profiling to the extent of regarding profiling as a dialogue between parents/carers, teachers and children.

This 'dialogue' is evident in the infant school mentioned above, as the following case study aims to illustrate.

Case study

It is 'Profiling Week' during the summer term at a large two-form-entry infant school with a nursery class and pre-school group (Stepping Stones) situated in the North West of England. A note had previously been sent to all parents, inviting them to come into school to select work for their own child's profile (Figure 3.2). The school has a long-established pattern of parental involvement and a whole-school commitment to working with parents. This type of invitation to share in their child's education is thus nothing new to these parents. They are also familiar with the concept of the 'profile', as many meetings have been held with them during the development of the scheme to ask their advice and to keep them informed. In addition to this, most of the parents have already taken part in a 'parental interview' during that term. At this session members of staff have shared a child's profile and National Curriculum records with the parent (except in the case of the nursery children, where the latter is not appropriate) and invited parents to contribute either verbally or in writing.

By 9.10 a.m. in one of the year 1 classrooms on the last day of 'Profiling Week', there was already a busy, relaxed atmosphere.

Figure 3.2 An invitation to parents to join in with 'Profiling Week'

Fifteen children were engaged in activities while the class teacher moved from table to table chatting to children and welcoming parents. As time progressed more children and parents arrived, some parents staying for a while, others leaving once their child was settled. Only five parents out of this class of 30 children had not already selected work for their child's profile during the hourly session available each morning for them to do so. Three of these parents now sat with their child selecting work. One of these parents was Suzanne.

Suzanne sat at a table with a group of children, a tray of work on her lap. Her child, Thomas, sat next to her building a mobilo model with the help of his friend. Suzanne looked carefully through each piece of work in Thomas's tray, occasionally asking him to explain a piece to her. She spoke positively to him throughout the exercise, saying 'That's nice, isn't it' and 'I like that' several times. Suzanne then took a hat which Thomas had made out of the tray, 'That's good', she said, putting it on his head and kissing him. Thomas smiled at his mum and replied 'It's a pirate hat', before returning to his model-making. When Suzanne had chosen a piece of work she showed it to Thomas, saying 'I've chosen this one, Thomas, because you have coloured it in neatly and it's a fireman. You want to be a fireman, don't you?' Thomas nodded in reply. Suzanne then recorded the reasons for her choice on the proforma, reading the words out to Thomas as she wrote. She then let Thomas choose a piece of work, and wrote his reason underneath hers. Thomas's teacher had already had a chat to her earlier in the week about writing down the reasons for her selection. By the time Suzanne had finished writing on the sheet Nancy, the class teacher, was kneeling next to her. Suzanne showed Nancy the two pieces of work which had been chosen and the completed proforma (Figure 3.3). 'That's great Suzanne, would you like to put it in his profile?' Nancy said, pointing to Thomas's profile which lay on a nearby table. Suzanne replied that she would, and the two women chatted generally about Thomas's progress. Suzanne then took the profile and had another quick glance at the contents before placing today's chosen work into it.

Since his mum had left, Thomas had played a maths game with two other children, completed his phonic worksheet from the day before, attended assembly and played outside. He was now sitting with five other children and his teacher, who told them that they

My work

date 18 June 1993

My mum/dad and me like this work.

My name ...Thomas.......................................

We like it because :-

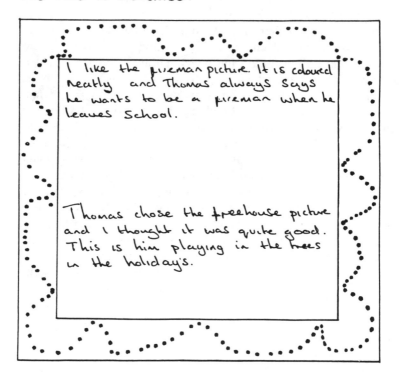

I like the fireman picture. It is coloured neatly and Thomas always says he wants to be a fireman when he leaves school.

Thomas chose the treehouse picture and I thought it was quite good. This is him playing in the trees in the holidays.

Figure 3.3 The proforma completed by Suzanne

were going to choose their favourite work to put in their profile folders. His teacher then went back to the other children in his class and talked to them before sending them off in groups to get on with their various tasks.

Thomas went off to get his tray of work which he had saved since September and on his return he put it on the table in front of him. 'I've chosen work already with my mum, now I'm going to do it on my own', Thomas told Charlene. 'I'm looking in all my folders', said Charlene, who had already got her tray. 'Seen all that work Thomas!' she exclaimed, pointing to the mound of paper in front of her. Thomas nodded in reply. 'Ashley, do you remember these?' remarked Thomas while putting his pirate hat on to his head. 'I can't find my pirate's hat', replied Ashley who was looking through his tray. 'I've got loads of work', said Paula to whoever cared to listen. 'So have I', came the excited reply from several children at the table.

Thomas looked through all of the work in his tray, lifting out some pieces as he went along and then he saw his dinosaur book. He looked carefully at the book then he put it on the table and returned his other work to the tray. He looked at his teacher, Nancy, who was sitting next to Paula and she beckoned him over. 'Have you chosen a piece of work Thomas?' she said to him. 'Yes this', replied Thomas, waving his dinosaur book at Nancy. 'Why have you chosen this piece of work?' 'Because it is good'. 'Why is it good?' asked Nancy. 'Because you said it was!' 'That was a long time ago, Thomas', Nancy replied. 'I remembered', said Thomas. 'Why else have you chosen this?' continued Nancy. 'Because I like it and it is neat'. 'Any other reasons?' 'No'. Nancy then gave Thomas a proforma and Thomas went away to record the reasons for his choice (Figure 3.4).

During the 45-minute session, all of the children in Thomas's group selected work to include in their profile folders. Ashley seemed to know which pieces of work he was looking for and he quickly found an observational drawing which he had completed three months previously and a letter which he had written seven months before. The reasons he gave for their selection were: 'The leaves are coloured in nicely. I have done neat writing. I like the letter and the stamp.' Charlene looked through all of her work first and then she returned to her pile to select a phonic worksheet. She had chosen this because 'It is coloured in neatly'; this was

Figure 3.4 The proforma completed by Thomas

significant to her due to the fact that 'Work is important'. Sam was the last to finish selecting his work. He looked through his work, lifting out pieces as he went along. Sam then examined carefully the six pieces which he had selected and finally chose three, among them a phonic worksheet on the letter 'S' because 'S is the beginning of my name' and a written record of the different ways in which he had used eight unifix cubes to make up his own 'sums' because 'I like adding up'. Sam commented that it had been difficult for him to choose his favourite work and to help him to do this he had 'Thought what I liked doing'.

In due course the class teacher will select a piece of work for each child's profile. She will use a range of criteria to aid this selection. A piece of work showing evidence of some of the following may be chosen:

- progress;
- effort;
- independent work;
- positive individual achievement.

This choice will then be shared with the child and the work placed in his/her profile.

The case-study material included so far provides only a snapshot of the whole process of profiling at the infant school in question. However, it may well have raised many issues for you which will most probably depend upon your professional priorities. The issues which it raises for me will be discussed under the following headings:

- A whole-school approach to profiling.
- Children and parents playing a major role in the assessment process.
- The selection of work for the profile.
- The influence of profiling on the teaching and learning process.

A whole-school approach to profiling

To be effective profiling should work through the whole school so that the arrangements for teaching, learning and profiling are complementary.

(Manchester City Council Education Department 1990)

The school has certainly taken on board this principle put forward by its local education authority. Profiling at the school is seen as a whole-school approach which has evolved over seven years and is still developing. The move towards profiling as a means of involving children and parents in the assessment process initially began when Chris, the deputy headteacher of the school, attended a course on profiling held by the LEA. The process was begun initially with the children in the reception class, who were encouraged to be critical and analytical about their work using a variety of strategies to develop the necessary skills. It would be easy to argue that these very young children would find this process difficult, but Chris was determined to try. She found that it was a valuable exercise in terms of: language development; encouraging logical and critical thinking; providing an insight into how the children learned; and strengthening relationships with individual children.

Convinced that this was a process well worth pursuing, the task to develop it into a whole-school approach began. In brief, this has taken much time, thought and energy; involving attendance at in-service sessions held by the LEA, many staff development days held at the school, individual interviews with members of staff, discussions at staff meetings, meetings and discussions with parents and the trialling of different methods and materials with the children. Consultation and training have been major issues for the management team and are seen as important elements in the development of a whole-school approach. This point is echoed by Janice Adams in Chapter 5 with reference to the development of an equal opportunities policy. The importance of staff development is also stressed by Evans (1986) who believes that this should be school-based, and by Hitchcock (1986: 32) who feels that it offers 'an opportunity to modify and adapt existing routine and the opportunity for cross fertilisation of ideas and experiences, and the chance to work in collaboration with others'. Indeed, the past seven years have seen a significant change in the assessment routines at the school, with a good deal of collaboration. The involvement of all staff in the development of a whole-school approach is crucial to ensure both a sense of ownership and to provide continuity for the children. This sense of ownership must also be extended to the parents and the children, particularly with the profiling process, as its success relies on their involvement. This issue will be discussed further in the following section.

The school has been careful not to let other pressures, for example the National Curriculum and its many requirements, push the profiling initiative to one side. In fact in many ways the two are able to go hand in hand. For example, reporting to parents and collecting evidence for teacher assessment are two requirements which are encompassed within the profiling process at the school. This is in line with the belief of Munby *et al.* (1989) that the harsher aspects of National Curriculum assessment arrangements can be 'humanized' by the use of profiles and records of achievement. The development of the profiling process has been a priority for the school and has been a feature of the school development plan. This is in line with the recommendation of HMI that 'the development and review of assessment policies should be a priority within school development plans' (DES 1992a: 35).

Seven years on, the school is now at a stage where a whole-school policy has been formulated and the profiling process begins in the 'Stepping Stones' pre-school group, continues in the nursery and then through the infant department. On transition to the junior school the child's National Curriculum records are automatically transferred, while parents and children are encouraged to show the profile, which is viewed as their property, to the junior school staff.

Without the continuity provided by the whole-school approach the profiling process would lack meaning and direction. It would not satisfy one of Manchester City Council Education Department's (1990) key purposes of profiling, which is to 'provide a range of evidence which shows progress over time'.

Although the whole-school policy has been formulated and agreed by staff the process of change does not stand still, nor should it if we are sensitive to the needs of children and families. Therefore areas for further development have been identified which are key issues affecting the quality and appropriateness of the assessment procedures in any establishment:

- the need for ongoing staff development and discussion to refine the process;
- the need for staff to develop interview techniques further, with the emphasis on being positive;
- the development of the format of the profile;
- the use of peer assessment.

Children and parents playing a major role in the assessment process

> All those involved in the children's learning should be involved in the assessments. This can mean all those working with the child at school, as well as the parents and the child.
>
> (Pidgeon 1992: 127)

This view is also held by Ritchie (1991), who believes that the involvement of the parent or carer and the child is an essential element of profiling. This is a valid point of view, but what does involvement really mean? As commented previously, it is not sufficient for the parent and child to just receive information about the child's learning. Real involvement would suggest these parties making valid contributions which are valued by the educarer. This point is echoed by the parent of one of the children already mentioned who commented:

> I like to be involved. It's important to be involved in your child's education. The way that they do it at this school has helped me to understand what Ashley does and to see the progress he has made through the year. I feel comfortable here, they don't make you feel stupid and they listen to you. It's good that we can choose work for the profile, it makes me feel that my point of view counts for something.

One could conclude from this statement that this parent is making a 'real' contribution and that this is valued by members of staff. What about Suzanne, the parent in the case study: to what extent do you feel that she has made a valid contribution to the assessment of her child's achievements?

Selecting work for the profile is not the only contribution that the parent or carer is able to make. Twice yearly the parents are invited to an interview/consultation with their child's class teacher to share views on the child's progress and to make a written contribution to the records. The nature of the school's relationship with the parents and the pattern of parental involvement also allow for many informal interactions with parents regarding children's progress and achievements. It would appear that at the school the involvement of parents and carers in the profiling process is enhanced by the quality of their relationships with the staff. As Chris

Marsh indicates in Chapter 7, successful relationships provide the basis for quality teaching and learning.

So what about staff relationships with the children, and to what extent are they involved? The case study would suggest that relationships between staff and children are relaxed, and that the points of view of the children, in relation to the reasons given for the selection of work, are accepted and valued.

Hitchcock (1986) makes the point that profiling can have a positive influence on relationships with children which can then improve the atmosphere in the classroom, thus increasing the children's attainment. Although this was stated with reference to pupils of secondary school age, it could be argued that it is just as relevant for younger children. As stated already, Chris, the deputy headteacher at the school, found that the profiling process strengthened her relationships with the children. In addition, another member of staff commented: 'Profiling is a good way of letting the child know that you are valuing what they are doing. I feel that it has helped me to get to know the children more. I definitely have a better relationship with them now.' The influence which this then has on the child's attainment will be discussed further towards the end of this chapter.

At the school in the case study, children are involved in the profiling process in a variety of ways. We have seen that they are given the opportunity to select work for their profiles. In addition to this, they are encouraged to have a degree of ownership of their own learning and to reflect upon and review their achievements regularly. The children are also able to comment upon and include evidence of achievements outside school if they wish.

The profile is viewed very much as the property of the child. During my many conversations with children of all ages at the school it became evident that they were proud of their profiles and really did view them as their own – recall Peter commenting 'it mine'. As the parent of one two-and-a-half-year-old told me: 'She'll sit for ages looking at it. "I done that", she'll say. She shows it other people. She's proud of it, they all are. It's a pity I didn't have anything like this when I was her age.' Ritchie (1991: 42) feels that this sense of ownership leads to an increase in commitment from children as they become more involved in the assessment process and their own learning.

Alongside the issue of ownership lie those concerning rights, trust, respect and control, sentiments which are also echoed by Gipps (1990) and Drummond (1993). If children are to 'own' their profile, should they feel that their educarers trust and respect their learning and their points of view? Should they have some control over their achievements?

One might question the feasibility of this ownership and control. For example, how can this ownership be reconciled with the need to pass on information to the adult at the child's next stage of learning? The infant school in question overcomes this by separating the legal requirements, for instance National Curriculum records, from the 'profile' at transition to the junior school. These are then sent to the child's year 3 teacher, and children encouraged to take their profile to show their new teacher. Before this, there is an understanding among children, staff and parents/carers that the profiles are housed at the school and passed through the school as appropriate.

At this particular school, the sense of ownership is extended to the parents. Profiles in all areas of the school are stored with easy access to children and parents, and the parents of the 'Stepping Stones' pre-school group are also encouraged to take the profiles home to update. The school feels strongly that parents also have the right of ownership and to be trusted in making contributions to the assessment process.

What about the issue of control? Are children really allowed to have control over their achievements and the profiling process, or is it purely a matter of paying lip-service to the notion? Perhaps this depends on the system used and the extent to which this is a result of negotiation among children, staff and parents/carers. For children of statutory school age, Ritchie (1991: 47) points out the further issue of how this fits in with the National Curriculum and its assessment procedures, over which children certainly do not have control. How these issues are reconciled takes us back to the first area for consideration, the need for a whole-school approach, which relies upon the ongoing discussion and refining of the profiling process.

The selection of work for the profile

As indicated previously, the selection of work for the profile is only one element of the whole profiling process. However, it is interesting to look closely at the reasons for selection given by children, parents/carers and staff.

The case study provides evidence that the children in the year 1 class selected work in different ways. For example, Charlene looked through all of her work first and then returned to her pile to select one piece, whereas Ashley seemed to know which pieces of work he was looking for. My research at the school indicates that children of all ages used a range of strategies to select work. Whatever the way in which the children selected the work, this was respected by the member of staff involved. Children were not told how to go about the process of selection in a prescriptive way but given help to develop the skills to enable them to do this however they chose. They are given the right to be individuals.

The reasons given for the selection of the work also differed, although there did seem to be a common theme of presentation. Many of the children in the case study used neatness and niceness as criteria for selection. Are they picking up adult values here to make judgements? In addition to this, a sense of achievement is apparent: phrases such as 'I tried hard', 'I like it' and 'It is good' spring to mind. There is evidence that the reasons given for selection do become more sophisticated the older the child is. One would hope that this is a result of engaging in the profiling process which enables the child to become more evaluative with experience. A further issue here seems to be the role of the adult in terms of questioning. In the case study Thomas told Nancy, his teacher, that he had chosen the dinosaur book because it was good. He was able to elaborate upon this answer when questioned further. Subsequent discussion with other members of staff also highlighted the importance of encouraging children to justify the reasons given for selection which seemed to increase their ability to be reflective and evaluative. Staff at the school feel that the reasons for selection given by the children provide valuable insights into individual children's learning styles and interests. This can then have a positive influence upon the teaching and learning process. As Ritchie (1991: 95) comments:

> Children's self-assessments are likely to provide teachers with feedback on the matching of task to child as well as to the appropriateness of the task in general. In this way

self-assessment can have a marked effect on the planning of the learning environment.

Discussion with Margaret, the headteacher of the school, who twice yearly looks at each child's profile, revealed that neat work was also of importance to the parent/carer: 'What comes over is that presentation for parents is important, content maybe not so much. Whereas with staff the content and the context are more important on the whole.' Why do you feel this may be so? To what extent is this use of different criteria an issue if we bear in mind the earlier comments about rights, trust, respect, ownership and control? At the moment the staff at the school do not share their reasons for selection with the parents as the latter make their selections before staff do so. Do you feel that staff should select pieces of work first so that the parent/carer can see what has been chosen by the staff member? Again, to what extent is this an issue if we respect the choices made by parents?

The type of work chosen is interesting. The majority of the year 1 children in the case study chose writing combined with drawing, or mathematics work. However, Peter and Melissa, the two younger children, had chosen mark-making, paintings and collage. Is this because to a young child painting is work? Does this view change as the child becomes older? Why? Why did Suzanne, the parent in the case study, not select the pirate hat which Thomas had made? After all, she did tell him that it was good. These observations raise questions concerning what adults and children view as work and have implications for the terminology which we as edu-carers use (see Chapter 2 for a discussion of the concept of 'play' into which some notions of 'work' can shade).

The influence of profiling on the teaching and learning process

As stated already, Murphy (1991) stresses the influence which profiles have on the teaching and learning process. This sentiment is also emphasized by many other writers, including Hitchcock (1986), Ritchie (1991) and Sutton (1991). This influence is evident at the infant school discussed in the case study.

It can be said that the profiling process is a positive experience for the children at the school. The opening comments of this chapter and the case study would suggest that the children enjoy the process. Peter and Melissa were both excited about sharing their profile with me and all the year 1 children were eager to select their work. But why is the profiling process such an enjoyable experience? Perhaps it is because there is an emphasis on the positives. Children at the school are encouraged to select their favourite work, parents and staff recognize and value the children's achievements and are able to present them with positive feedback. This is very much in line with the view stated by the Manchester City Council Education Department (1990) that 'The child needs to feel that the profile positively reflects her/his performance'.

Does every child not have a right to be treated and viewed positively and with respect? As Drummond (1993: 186) argues: 'Assessment practices that contribute, however minutely, to a learner's sense of personal failure cannot be justified. All pupils are learners; their rights to learn and to feel that their teachers trust and respect their learning are paramount.' The profiling process at the school in question does seem to enable staff and parents to respect the child's learning. Achievements are viewed positively, and there is an emphasis on what the child can rather than cannot do. Children at the school are seen as individuals with a valid point of view. They are encouraged to develop this point of view via the selection of work for the profile and the ongoing evaluation of activities. This process is begun in the Stepping Stones pre-school group, where children are encouraged to comment upon what they enjoyed most about particular sessions, and is built upon throughout the school. Profiling is used as a means of helping children to develop as critical thinkers which in turn can have a marked effect upon the learning process. It is widely recognized (Broadfoot 1986; Gipps 1990; Ritchie 1991; Hitchcock 1993) that profiling can significantly influence motivation, self-esteem, confidence and attitudes to learning.

In conclusion

This is by no means an exhaustive account of the profiling process, nor is it a definitive discussion of the issues which it raises. It is hoped, however, that it has set you thinking about your own views on assessment and on your assessment practices. As Drummond and Nutbrown (1992: 103) sum up:

Assessment is a process that must enhance [children's] lives, their learning and development. The educators' needs are secondary to those of the children they work with. Assessment must work for children. Their minds and their futures are entrusted to our hands for the brief years of childhood. We must do all in our power to serve them well.

Questions for discussion

The following questions may help you to reflect further upon your current practice and beliefs.

The workplace

1 What opportunities are available for staff to discuss their philosophies and beliefs?
2 Does your workplace have a shared philosophy with regard to assessment?
3 In what ways can this philosophy be developed?
4 To what extent do the assessment procedures used in your workplace provide continuity in approach?
5 How can this be developed?

The parent/carer

6 What strategies do you use to involve the parent/carer in the assessment process?
7 Are there any ways in which you can build upon this practice?
8 To what extent does it allow the parent/carer to make a valid contribution?
9 In what ways do you consult parents when changing or refining the assessment process?
10 What rights do you feel parents should have in the assessment process?

The child

11 What rights do you feel a child should have with regard to assessment?
12 In what way do your assessment records provide a picture of the 'whole child' rather than just his/her academic attainment?

13 Have you consulted the child about what is to be included in the record?
14 To what extent is the child involved in contributing to the record?
15 Who do you feel should own the record?
16 How important do you think it is to help the child develop skills of evaluation and reflection?
17 In what ways can you do this?

Suggestions for further reading

Blenkin, G.M. and Kelly, A.V. (eds) (1992) *Assessment in Early Childhood Education.* London: Paul Chapman.
Drummond, M.J., Rouse, D. and Pugh, G. (1992) *Making Assessment Work. Values and Principles in Assessing Young Children's Learning.* Nottingham: Nottingham Educational Suppliers, Arnold and National Children's Bureau.
Drummond, M.J. (1993) *Assessing Children's Learning.* London: David Fulton.
Ritchie, R. (ed.) (1991) *Profiling in Primary Schools: A Handbook for Teachers.* London: Cassell.

4

'It's nice here, now': Managing young children's behaviour

Sylvia Phillips

> What is of prime importance is that the curriculum . . . should
> be experienced in an environment which fosters the develop-
> ment of social relationships and positive attitudes to learning
> and behaviour . . .
>
> (DES 1990: 9)

Earlier chapters have shown how children's relationships with each
other and with their teachers and other adults can be encouraged
and nurtured by an appropriate curriculum. Providing opportunities to play and work co-operatively, supported by sensitive intervention from adults, is essential in planning the curriculum for the
early years. Teachers plan activities to enable children to discover
that learning is worthwhile and enjoyable, in the hope that therefore they will want to learn. They pay particular attention not only
to the aims and nature of activities, but also to the organization of
learning spaces, use of resources and how children will be grouped
for learning. These aspects of the learning environment, including
deployment of adults, use of display and the way in which children's achievements are acknowledged all contribute to an environment which promotes the development of social relationships
and positive attitudes – a learning environment of *quality*.

However, teachers find that the planning for such an environment which appears successful in many schools and nurseries does
not achieve the same outcomes in others. This is particularly true
where teachers report an apparent increase in the number of very

young children who enter nursery or school 'unable' to form relationships, who appear 'unwilling' to learn and who 'lack the skills for learning'. A great many of these children are described as presenting very aggressive behaviours which not only prevent them from learning, but also hinder the learning opportunities of other children. Their behaviours present new challenges to many teachers of young children who have, perhaps, previously only encountered such behaviour occasionally. Although arguments continue about whether or not there is a real increase in aggressive behaviour, research undertaken for the Elton Report (DES 1989a) showed that over 74 per cent of the primary teachers in their sample had dealt with acts of physical aggression between pupils over a one-week period and 17 per cent had dealt with them on a daily basis.

Elton reported: 'A number of submissions to us suggest that this behaviour is becoming more common among young children' (DES 1989a: 134). Where such behaviours are encountered and the adults have difficulty in maintaining a peaceful, happy environment, the quality of learning is inevitably threatened. In particular, it is difficult both to foster social relationships and to present 'learning' as enjoyable. Many teachers respond either by feeling guilty and inadequate or by 'rejecting' some children, believing they must have such complex problem behaviours that they cannot be taught in a mainstream setting. There is some support for these reactions. Research into 'effective' primary schools (Mortimore *et al.* 1988) showed that, given similar pupil populations from similar catchment areas, some schools not only managed behaviour more effectively but also appeared to be able to prevent disruption. Elton claimed that 'good schools can reduce misbehaviour to an absolute minimum' (DES 1989a: 66), and an HMI report (1987) made similar observations. Elton later implies that the behaviour of all but a few children can be 'managed' by teachers, but that: 'A small minority of pupils have such severe and persistent behaviour problems as a result of emotional, psychological or neurological disturbance that their needs cannot be met in mainstream schools' (DES 1989a: 150).

This chapter explores how teachers, encouraged by research which shows that they can 'make a difference', might work in a setting where many children present difficult, disruptive and antisocial behaviours to provide the sort of environment recommended in the Rumbold Report. It presents a case study of a nursery which had undertaken an extensive review of its curriculum over two years, reorganizing how it grouped children, used space and deployed resources in relation to planned activities. There had been extensive staff training in curriculum development, particularly in the area of play. Teachers were now concerned that some children were still unable to profit from the curriculum because of their own or other children's emotional and behaviour difficulties.

The study points to several key issues for discussion by teachers and students, including those of methods of behaviour management, the need for whole-school policies and working in partnership with parents or carers.

Case study

The school

The case study is based on a nursery school for children aged from three to five, situated in an area of mixed housing, although the majority of children come from council houses and flats. There is high unemployment in the area, which has a local reputation for theft and violence. There are many single-parent families, where there is a pattern of young mothers who become involved in successive short-term relationships with 'stepfathers/uncles'. However, there is a reasonably stable population, with extended families of grandparents, uncles and aunts living in the same neighbourhood. The teachers, nursery nurses and lunchtime organizers who have been some years in the school know several family histories well, and the school has developed good relationships with a majority of parents. When these more established (and usually older) staff claim that 'behaviour is getting worse in young children in the school', staff who have arrived more recently listen respectfully. When they hear even very experienced staff say that they do not know how to cope with the behaviours of some children, recently qualified teachers feel both some relief (that if they are not coping at least it may not be because of personal failure) and some anxiety in that there appears to be no source of expertise available to them in the school.

The nursery is organized in home groups of about 12–15 children, each with a marked-out base and carpeted area, and each with its own teacher and nursery nurse. In addition, there are three non-attached nursery nurses who have designated responsibilities across groups and activities, and there are four special support assistants (SSAs) who are specifically there to give individual support to four children with statements for special educational needs (SEN). These children all have severe learning difficulties, one also has cerebral palsy and severe speech difficulties and one has a profound hearing loss. The children with SEN all participate fully in the nursery's activities, and teachers have welcomed them into the school. The staff has been very stable until two or three years ago, when one teacher left for promotion and was replaced by a newly qualified teacher who left after a year for 'an easier school' and was in turn replaced by another newly qualified teacher. Five of the nursery nurses have been appointed in the last two years – again there have been several changes within this group of five as some 'came and left quickly'. However, the current staff are all very committed to teaching in this school and share a strong belief in the value of nursery education 'particularly for children in this sort of area'.

Thus when the deputy headteacher commented one day on the regularity of complaints and grumbles about children's behaviour which she heard in the staffroom, there was full support for targeting 'dealing with problem behaviour' as an area for staff development. A teacher attending a local in-service course on behaviour management agreed to act as facilitator and also to seek advice from her tutor.

Sharing concerns

Three major concerns were identified:

- the fact that certain behaviours inhibited learning and disrupted the learning of other children, particularly because adult attention was diverted to deal with misbehaviour;
- the atmosphere in the nursery was often tense and stressful both for children and adults, and therefore not conducive to learning;
- teachers and nursery nurses alike felt inadequate to deal with many of the behaviours and this put them under further stress.

First steps: defining the 'problem'

An initial step was for all the adults to describe and discuss pupils whose behaviours they encountered most frequently and found difficult to deal with. This session proved useful in leading to shared policy-making, as many agreed it was 'a relief' just to admit to the problems. Some agreed that it also gave 'a sense of proportion' in that some of these behaviours which were most challenging and difficult to manage were (fortunately) not as frequent as at first thought – it was 'a sense of hopelessness in not knowing what to do that makes it seem never-ending' (as one teacher said). The most experienced teacher listed 'James, who is always hitting other children and spitting and kicking; Brian, Ashley, Peter and Martin . . . very aggressive to other children, hit and kick and are rude and defiant even to me'. Her nursery nurse said: 'Don't forget Stephen, he's a really awkward and strange little boy'. This accounted for six of the eight boys in one group of 12 children.

A list was made of all the behaviours staff (including lunchtime organizers) felt disrupted learning. This included:

- Defying or challenging adults, often replying 'I won't' when asked to do something. One group of 4 three-year-olds lay down on the floor and refused to join in a singing game, and then 'laughed and giggled' at the teacher.
- Fighting other children (particularly in the playground; in the toilets area; in 'play' and 'choosing' situations).
- Running round the room and interfering with other children's work – knocking over constructions, tearing paintings, and so on.
- Swearing.
- Poking, hitting and pinching/'nipping' other children – often 'surreptitiously', during story-time and group activities.
- Spitting, biting, kicking.
- Shouting out/interrupting other children or an adult during group work.
- Hiding the property of other children.

Systematic observation and recording over a two-week period found that such incidents were far from continuous, although every teacher and nursery nurse recorded at least one incident in the above categories every day. As the surveys conducted for the Elton

Report showed, the most severe cases of physical aggression occurred in the playground and less-structured activities. It was also noted that boys were more likely to be physically aggressive than girls, although there were some girls, like four-year-olds Debbie and Laura who hit, scratched and bit others (both boys and girls). The boys, however, usually hit only other boys, although they 'pushed', swore and were verbally abusive towards both boys and girls. Asked to try to identify some of the more 'positive' aspects of the children identified as aggressive, the staff agreed that they had never seen any pupils being aggressive towards any of the children with SEN. While some 'ignored' their presence, others were seen to go to pains to help the four children.

Both teachers and nursery nurses were particularly concerned when children openly challenged and defied their authority. Every member of staff described at least one incident of a child who said 'I won't' or 'lies on the floor and says "won't"' or 'stands and stares insolently'. These were the behaviours they found most difficult to deal with and admitted to a range of inconsistent responses, varying from prolonging the confrontation – 'Oh, yes, you will' – to nagging, pleading, threatening, ignoring or trying to 'laugh it off'. They described their feelings of frustration, powerlessness and inadequacy when in this situation and also when intervening unsuccessfully in other situations. It was the fear of failing to be seen to be effective by other children which often led to a policy of non-intervention. This also provoked a feeling of guilt, because they felt that not only might other children lose respect for them as adults, but also might be more easily intimidated by children they believed adults could not manage.

While the most heated discussion centred on these misbehaviours, teachers also identified other behaviours which lead to ineffective learning, among them poor concentration, the inability to sit still for long, not listening, inability to play, attention-seeking and poor language skills.

Most staff believed that the major contributory factors to all behaviours which affect learning in the nursery are inconsistent handling in the home and a lack of good models of relationships built on mutual respect. Other contributory factors were cited as: 'violence on TV and videos; too much time watching videos; no positive interaction with adults; poverty; no talking and conversation between child and adults in the home; neglect; the culture of the community; poor handling by lunchtime supervisors; inconsistent handling in school; lack of training for teachers of young children in how to manage children with behaviour problems; certain critical situations in school life, such as coming into and leaving the nursery; any situation where children line up or sit down in groups larger than about 6; "exciting events", such as when the community policeman brings in a police dog; wet and windy days'. In addition, particular children might be affected by short- or long-term factors in the home and family.

Examining practices

Staff were also very aware of the way in which their own behaviour might affect the learning environment and create or at least reinforce a *negative* ethos. This anxiety had been raised at a very early stage, and during the period when staff recorded incidents of misbehaviour three teachers had kept a tally of their use of negative statements, gestures and actions and, later, of their positive strategies. This activity, suggested by the teacher-facilitator, was based on the 'Positive Teaching' programme of Wheldall and Merrett (1985). All three teachers were surprised by the frequency of their negative comments: 'Don't do that'; 'Not you again, James'; 'I might have guessed it would be you, Lisa. You're a very naughty girl'; 'You're a selfish little boy. No wonder no one likes you'. They felt ambivalent about describing as negative statements which they felt they made politely or with humour: 'That's enough, please'; 'You little monkey/monster' – but agreed that within the total context they were 'negative' rather than 'positive'.

Certain interesting aspects were noted:

- They used more 'negatives' in less-structured situations, than when, for instance, leading small-group activities. This may reflect uncertainty about eventualities where fear or anticipation of possible troubles leads to a teacher needing to use expressions which 'demonstrate' control.
- Planned and controlled situations showed not only a reduction in use of 'negatives' but also greater use of positive statements.
- 'Negatives' were used more about *behaviour* and how children related to each other: 'Get on with your own work, Brian'; 'Leave Ashley alone'. 'Positives' tended to be used for learning and

learning outcomes: 'That is a lovely drawing, Rachel'; 'Yes, we call it blue, Brian. Well done'. Only rarely was a child told his work was 'untidy'.

• Their findings tended to support research that teachers often reinforce misbehaviour, by paying a lot of attention to it, even through negative statements, rather than praising and reinforcing good behaviours. This appears to reflect the fact that we expect the norm to be good/conforming behaviour.

Sharing goals

These discussions led naturally to agreement that the staff should work together to produce a more positive ethos and, having discussed what behaviours they did not find acceptable, that they should determine which behaviours they did wish to encourage. They agreed that part of their approach would be to employ, at all times, the technique of 'Catch Them Being Good' described in several texts on behaviour management (Montgomery 1989), which meant that when they observed a child behaving appropriately they would praise the child, drawing attention to the 'good behaviour'.

They identified 'desirable behaviours' by listing

What we want children to do:
• play together
• share
• wait for others
• take turns
• be kind to others
• do what the adults in school ask.

Following recommendations from the HMI Report (1987) and guidelines on devising Positive School Discipline Plans (for example, from Galvin *et al.* 1990), they reviewed the rewards and sanctions used in the nursery. Some staff were unhappy about the use of sanctions for very young children, particularly the use of the extreme sanction which would be to refuse to accept a child for a day. Following consultations with parents, however, this was finally agreed, and a graduated list of sanctions relating to severity and frequency of misbehaviours was drawn up. A written policy followed showing what behaviours were required (as good behaviours) and which behaviours were not acceptable. The policy showed how good behaviour would be reinforced and rewarded and how unacceptable behaviour would be discouraged.

There was also, here, a full discussion about the use of touch. Physical touch, on the hand, arm or shoulder, often has a positive and calming effect on a child; it can be used, for example, to denote friendly contact, or to sustain a relationship even while speaking to another child. Similarly, many adults point to the benefits of giving a child a 'cuddle'. Staff were very conscious of the problem of false allegations of abuse and most felt they could no longer put an arm round a child or give a cuddle – particularly to some of the aggressive, 'anti-social' children whom they felt might benefit from physical contact, but be most likely to make allegations about abuse.

It was agreed to develop strategies which:

- clearly distinguished acceptable and non-acceptable behaviours for the children;
- separated the action (or behaviour) from the child;
- reduced teacher stress and could prevent adults from becoming so emotional that they shouted or nagged or repeated themselves ineffectively;
- could be applied consistently;
- could be agreed by all adults so they not only benefited from support of others but were seen to be working co-operatively by children;
- demonstrated that children were valued and respected;
- offered a safe and secure framework where adults were seen to be reliable and trustworthy;
- protected the 'right to learn' of all children;
- demonstrated the authority of the teacher/adult in the nursery.

It was decided to avoid the use of 'star charts' except where a child might be on an individual programme, and to emphasize the use of teacher praise. It was agreed that praise would be given in a specific way so that the child knew *what* was being praised: 'That was very kind, Jayne, lending James your pencil'.

Dealing with conflict between pupils was a major concern, whether this was a dispute over ownership – 'That Lego's mine' – or unprovoked physical aggression.

Using the principles outlined above, the staff agreed to employ

Table 4.1 Routine adopted by the nursery for the management of aggression

---

1 Child identified as the aggressor is led (gently) away from the action by whichever adult is nearest.

2 Child talked to 'quietly and privately' using a standard pattern of words.
'That was (adjective to describe the behaviour).'
Four adjectives were agreed as appropriate to help very young children understand that the behaviour was wrong:

DANGEROUS, SILLY, UNKIND, AWFUL

(Others had been suggested including bad, mean, greedy.) No explanation is asked for. We don't really want to know why. Does a child always know – or provide an answer we accept and 'excuse' the behaviour?

3 No apology is sought. If the child says s/he's sorry, or seems sorry, the adult says:
'As you're sorry, you can go back now.
But please don't do that again'.

4 If s/he repeats the behaviour, or doesn't seem sorry, the adult says:
'That was dangerous. Next time you do that you will *sit on the chair.*'
The staff agreed to have a 'naughty' chair in each base, so that this became the sanction. They sat on it for two minutes and then rejoined when the adult told them 'You can go back now. But please don't do that again'. (The adult does not ask the child to apologize or agree s/he's been naughty).

5 If the act is repeated, the teacher says:
'That was   . You will now sit on the chair'.

---

a routine (Table 4.1) minimizing the use of language and so controlling some of the emotional outpourings which can occur in such situations. What was important was to show that the teacher was in control. Very few children did not comply (despite teachers' earlier anxieties about defiance), but if they did then another routine was used where one of the other adults would lead the child away to a different group base for a short time. These methods proved very effective in decreasing both aggressive and defiant behaviours.

Extending the range of strategies

At the same time staff increased their use of 'positive' statements for acceptable behaviours. They did not restrict the adjectives used here, but tried to specify an act – 'That was kind, lending Rachel your book' – and use smiles, 'thumbs-up' and colloquial expressions of praise or pleasure. Children were encouraged to comment positively on each other's work.

The staff also developed a strategy for helping children to behave appropriately in situations which had often provoked conflict, particularly to encourage 'sharing' and 'taking turns'. An example was when Ashley wanted to use the telephone in the shop, but Jon was already using it. He was encouraged to tell an adult instead of his previous behaviour of snatching it or fighting for it, and she would lead him by the hand saying 'Come with me and we'll ask Jon if you can have a turn now'. Children soon used the modelled language. As long as a child had not just begun to use the equipment (in which case a time limit was put on the turn), the adult could ensure a polite exchange. There is learning here for both children. Turn-taking involves not only learning how to ask or intervene 'politely' but also how to 'relinquish', whether in playing, using equipment or in a conversation.

High priority had been given, during their recent curriculum review, to the language curriculum – particularly speaking and listening skills. Many of the children entering nursery at three or four were described as having the language development of much younger children, and great value was placed on extending language use. A review of their curriculum documents and record system showed an emphasis on the language of concept development (for example, colour, size, shape), on the classification of nouns (for example, labelling for parts of the body, objects in the nursery and home, clothes) and on the development of sentence structures. They now incorporated greater use of language to describe and explain feelings and attitudes and examined how picture and story books already in the nursery could be used to emphasize acceptable behaviours, relationships between people, feelings, values and attitudes. They also used the normal curriculum

activities and materials to help children talk more about themselves and explore the self in relation to others, often adapting
materials designed for older children such as the Sharp-Eye
Materials 'Me and Myself' (Ruel 1989).

Working co-operatively

Many staff found it difficult at first to structure their language so
carefully in situations fraught with emotion. Some also found it
difficult to make more positive statements. However, the fact that
all the staff were involved made it easier – the adults had adult
models! – and some change in ethos was noted within two to three
weeks. As one teacher put it: 'I find myself smiling naturally now.'
Increasingly they found ways of using the everyday curriculum
as a vehicle for fostering relationships, self-image and involving
children in learning. They felt, however, that this was only possible because they had been able to reduce the incidence of misbehaviour. A comment from one of the children summed up the
change: 'It's nice here, now.'

Summary

Initially these teachers sought to establish a good learning environment by seeking 'management techniques' which they hoped
could be applied and would result in well-behaved, compliant
children 'ready to learn'. They found that there is a range of
management strategies for reducing disruption and promoting
desirable behaviours. However, as they examined their situation
and children's needs in relation to what they perceived were essential conditions for learning, they concluded that the curriculum
and learning experiences could not be separated from 'behaviour'.

The case study provides evidence that a learning environment
which fosters social relationships and positive attitudes to learning
and behaviour can be engendered and maintained through the
curriculum itself rather than being seen as a precondition.

The Elton Report's first recommendation was that all teachers
should receive training in managing pupils' behaviour, and it is
clear that where there is a high incidence of inappropriate behaviours, teaching and learning are disrupted. However, it is not

sufficient to try to remove unwanted behaviours: we have to decide what behaviours we want to encourage.

Certain important issues arise from the case study:

- How do adults decide which behaviours are appropriate?
- To what extent does behaviour management of children involve the adults in questioning their own values and practices, and possibly having to change the way they teach, organize learning and even use language? Pollard and Tann (1987) provide some good examples of this sort of reflective practice.
- What is the relationship between adult decision-making, the application of social norms via a set of classroom rules and the encouragement of individual personality development?
- How important is it for a policy to be nursery-wide? No matter which adult was encountered (or heard about!) in this nursery, children met the same warmth and concern and knew what adults' expectations were. Mutual support was also very important for the staff, whose chosen methods meant they had to exercise careful control over their own behaviour and language at the very times when it was easy to act emotionally, that is, when they were being challenged by very emotional children.
- Does concern about managing groups and disruption mean that the needs of some of the children with more deep-seated emotional difficulties are neglected? It could be argued that it does. However, as the adults in the nursery began to spend less time on control and discipline, they had more time to interact with and support individual children. They could observe them closely, discovering more about their learning strengths and difficulties and also their anxieties and concerns. They were able to identify those needing further assessment and ask for an educational psychologist's advice.

There are many approaches to behaviour management, and these are not the concern of this book. Further reading is recommended at the end of the chapter.

It is also important to state that this case study does not do justice to the extent to which parents were involved in this nursery, as working with parents is covered in another chapter. Not only were parents involved in drawing up the policy, but there were also group sessions to help them to deal more effectively with their children at home. There can be a tendency to 'blame' parents for their children's behaviour, or call them to a school to complain about a child without finding out whether the same behaviours also exist at home where they may be a source of stress in the home rather than a product. Parents need support – not to be made to feel inadequate.

A further issue in the study concerns the relationship between the school and its values and those of the surrounding community. Teachers in this nursery agreed there was dissonance, but felt it necessary to establish a safe, secure learning environment even if it was 'isolated' from the outside world. It is important to consider this issue in determining a behaviour policy, and particularly when deciding how to encourage social development.

Co-operation, respect for self and others and rejection of violence and aggression were valued in the school but not necessarily in the homes of all the children. The teachers agreed that they should not impair children's relationships with parents and their 'outside world' and so would try not to make 'careless' remarks which carried implicit criticism of family or home: 'You might do that at home, but not here' or 'I don't care if your Mum does say you can, I say you can't'. In setting out the requirements for 'good behaviour' reference was always in terms of the nursery premises. Thus they established acceptable behaviours for the playground, listening to stories and so on, in addition to the more general acceptable social behaviours. They taught children that 'behaviour' is sometimes situation-specific but that there are certain overriding principles.

Let us look at some of the issues raised in this study concerning how the staff fostered the development of social relationships. Their goals for acceptable behaviours clearly emphasize two aspects concerning sharing and turn-taking. Staff also believed that in order to relate to others, a child needs not only models of relationships but also a sense of identity and self-worth in order to know how to relate to others. They believed (and we could question their grounds) that many of the nursery's children had no real sense of identity and had low self-esteem because they had not been handled consistently and respected as individuals by those who were their 'significant others' (that is, parents/carers).

The teachers' strategies are supported by theories which propose that self-concept develops through our perceptions of the way 'significant others' behave towards us. Self-concept influences not only how we feel about ourselves but also feelings and behaviour towards others. Part of this picture is our 'self-esteem' which is concerned with how 'worthy' we feel we are, in comparison with 'ideal self' which is either the sort of person we would like to be or perhaps what we think others would like us to be. If children are to enter into successful social relationships and become confident about approaching learning, they must have a sense of self including self-in-a-learning-context and a sense of self-worth and value. The work of Carl Rogers (1951) has suggested that if teachers show empathy, unconditional positive regard and genuineness then self-esteem can be raised and the individual can develop and learn freely. These qualities can be seen in the teachers' approaches, although several admitted that they found difficulty in demonstrating 'positive regard' to children who misbehaved. Here their very structured approach of labelling the act, not the child, was important.

Gaining a sense of identity and feeling of self-worth is important not only for developing relations with others but also for fostering a positive attitude towards learning. It is important to arrange experiences where there are more opportunities to succeed than to fail, but in attempting to raise self-esteem we may be tempted to try to prevent children from failing! If children are to find enjoyment in learning, then they must discover how to experiment, to live with uncertainties, to 'fail' without feeling a 'failure', and how to cope with frustration. The importance of an adult model working in 'parallel' with children and voicing his/her own experiences is very useful. For some children this may be essential. Similarly, if children feel they are in a secure environment, where warmth and praise are more common than negative criticism, they will be more likely to investigate unknowns.

Clearly there is a close connection between development of 'self' and the development of social relationships. Early Piagetian theory distinguished two aspects of how young children begin to develop social awareness, particularly in relation to 'morality', which are pertinent to the development of social relationships. These are through notions of *constraints*, whereby adults may impose rules, and *reciprocity*, where a child and 'another' submit their own rules and negotiate how they will interact. These are both important in developing social knowledge, although to present them as categories of methods may be questionable. However, the adults in this situation perceived a need for clear limits and constraints in order to provide a positive learning environment (including 'rules' provided by modelling, for how one person approaches another in order to establish positions for negotiation). The importance of reciprocity in a relationship was indicated by the way the staff offered models of how to relate to each other. The teachers placed great emphasis on the importance of language in exploring one's own feelings and also in communicating with others. The case study provided an example of an adult modelling how to interrupt another child's activity and *ask* for a turn.

Do we give sufficient attention to fostering young children's language development in relation to their social and emotional development? Is there often a greater emphasis on the language of the school and cognitive development? We emphasize the value of play in learning, including cognitive learning, yet, as the Elton Report noted, 'some of the children now entering nursery and reception classes lack the basic skills needed to talk to and play with other children' (DES 1989a: 134).

Chazan *et al.* (1983: 60) draw attention to the fact that where behavioural difficulties are not very pronounced, then making 'fairly slight changes to your ordinary pattern of work' can help to overcome problems. They emphasize the use of creative activities and language development in particular. They claim that 'although interaction with others is not entirely dependent on verbal communication, it does not greatly progress without language' (Chazan *et al.* 1983: 68). They identify six particular ways in which language can aid emotional and social development:

1 Language helps children to regulate their own behaviour and that of others.
2 Language facilitates *the development of a concept of self.*
3 Language influences *the development of attitudes.*
4 Language helps the child to *an increasing understanding of the feelings and reactions of other adults and children.*
5 Language enables children *to express* themselves emotionally and socially in play to a fuller extent than is possible without it. [It] helps the development of complex and imaginative forms of play which might otherwise remain at a low level.

6 Language assists the child to become *aware that there is more than one possible response* to most situations.

(Chazan *et al.* 1983: 68–69; emphasis in original)

Adult–child conversation is another way of providing models of language within a natural context. Adult–child conversation not only can be a way of extending language but also boosts self-esteem by giving time to children and showing that what they have to say is worth listening to. A single conversation can involve the use of language in all the ways listed above. Yet Sylva *et al.* (1980), in the Oxford Pre-school Research Project, found little evidence of sustained conversation between children and adults or among children themselves. In this nursery the adults were aware of entering into longer periods of talk with children when they were less anxious about maintaining general discipline. However, analysis of one or two 'conversations' showed they tended to follow a pattern of teacher asking a question, child responding, teacher making a comment extending child's utterance or giving approval.

This form of language use is usually a direct result of the teacher's aim to foster the pupil's language development. Bruner used the term 'scaffolding' to describe the assistance which may be offered to help children achieve by structuring their presentation and through careful use of language (Sugden 1989). Careful intervention is required to offer minimal but helpful support so that the child is led to make his/her own responses. This is what all teachers of young children hope to do when they interact in learning situations, but it requires considerable skill. Its use is particularly relevant where young children perhaps have difficulties in learning or have not yet developed positive attitudes towards learning as in this nursery. Several studies demonstrating successful use of 'scaffolding' with such children may be found in Sugden (1989).

Chapter 2 emphasizes the value of play, yet some children, Elton claims, may be unable to reap these benefits when they first come to school (DES 1989a). Should play be taught? The nursery staff provided adult models in play situations initially to model behaviour. Some staff were reluctant to join in at first, and many of them believed that play should be left entirely for children's own exploration although agreeing that adults should provide the structure and resources for its development. Similar reluctance was noted by Bruner (1980) in the Oxford Pre-school Research Project.

Chazan *et al.* (1983) advocate strongly that adults must be 'active participants' in play, particularly where children have social and emotional difficulties. They point particularly to the way in which play helps children become better problem-solvers, learning to predict outcomes and appreciate their effects on others and feel the results of others' actions on themselves. Where these areas are problematic for some children, adult intervention and modelling appears essential.

The emphasis placed on language development highlights a further issue. When we identify 'needs' and establish teaching goals, is there a tendency to over-react and forget 'normal' development and behaviours? In the case of language development and encouraging 'social talk' and extending 'language for learning' do we sometimes use too much talk? It is important to remember the value of working independently and in parallel, including maintaining a 'companionable silence'. I am mindful of a three-year-old once saying to me: 'Will you please stop talking? My brain is trying to think.'

Similarly, when we seek to foster the development of social relationships for children perceived as anti-social or asocial, we should not set an unrealistic aim of requiring co-operative group work all the time. Children of three and four need to be able to work or play on their own, in parallel and in groups at different times and for different purposes. Indeed, Sylva *et al.* (1980) found young children rarely played imaginatively in groups of more than two unless an adult intervened. While it is important, therefore, to demonstrate how to approach others, to share and 'take turns', it is also important to teach 'non-interference' with other children and to show, perhaps through silent parallel play, or with very little self-commentary, that there is value and enjoyment in solitary activity.

The teachers in this study attempted to be sensitive to the needs of both individuals and the group, and were prepared to review their own teaching. While some readers may question the details of the methods they employed, the case study shows how staff developed strategies to manage children's behaviour in ways which offered support for them to learn how to work more co-operatively and develop relationships with other children and adults in the nursery. For this to occur it was vital to develop a warm, positive ethos within which children could feel safe and secure. Attention was paid to improving the children's self-concepts and demonstrating that the children were valued by adults and should learn to value each other. If children are to find enjoyment in learning then they must learn to try things out, to 'fail' without feeling they are 'failures', to be encouraged to experiment and enquire.

Teachers, too, need to feel confident in their teaching and to experience successful outcomes to their planning. The case study shows a staff who grew in confidence when they found that planning to manage children's behaviour not only reduced disruption, but also gave them the feeling they were in control of the learning situation and able to avoid the stress which arises when making *ad hoc* responses to disruptive incidents with the uncertainties of effectiveness that entails.

It may be the case that only when staff have high self-esteem and enjoy co-operative working relationships can they really provide a learning environment of quality.

Points, issues and questions for discussion

1 What sorts of behaviour do you find difficult to manage? Why?
2 If you were faced with the same sorts of challenge as the teachers in this nursery, how might you respond? What actions would you take that might be different from those they took? Discuss the reasons for your approach.
3 Draw up a list of behaviours you consider to be *inappropriate* for very young children and a list of behaviours you regard to be appropriate or desirable. Share practices with colleagues and discuss whether there is a tendency to tell children what they *should not* do, rather than make explicit what they *should* do. How might teachers guide and support children towards appropriate behaviours? Discuss ways in which you reinforce 'appropriate' behaviour rather than inappropriate behaviour. What 'reward systems' do you use?
4 Discuss specific ways in which play, drama and language development strategies, offered within the normal curriculum in a nursery or infant school, might be used to help all children to learn to:
   • co-operate with others;

- control their own behaviour;
- deal with frustration;
- explore their own feelings;
- explore the feelings of others;
- solve 'problems'.

5 Identify some of the ways in which teachers and other adults in schools and nursery centres might try to raise children's self-esteem.

Suggested further reading

Bury LEA (1993) *Mudpack (Managing Unwanted Disruption)*.

Chazan, M., Laing, A.F., Jones, J., Harper, G.C. and Bolton, J. (1983) *Helping Young Children with Behaviour Difficulties*. London: Croom Helm.

Douglas, J. (ed.) (1990) *Emotional and Behavioural Problems in Young Children: A Multidisciplinary Approach to Identification and Management*. Windsor: NFER/Nelson.

Galvin, P., Mercer, S. and Costa, P. (1990) *Building a Better-Behaved School*. London: Longman.

Behaviour management

Blatchford, P. (1989) *Playtime in the Primary School: Problems and Improvements*. Windsor: NFER/Nelson.

Cheeseman, P.L. and Watts, P.E. (1985) *Positive Behaviour Management: A Manual for Teachers*. London: Croom Helm.

Docking, J. (1990) *Managing Behaviour in the Primary School*. London: David Fulton.

McManus, M. (1989) *Troublesome Behaviour in the Classroom: A Teachers' Survival Guide*. London: Routledge.

Merrett, F. and Wheldall, K. (1990) *Positive Teaching in the Primary School*. London: Paul Chapman.

Building self-esteem

Borba, M. and Borba, C. (1978) *Self Esteem: A Classroom Affair: Vol. I*. San Francisco: Harper.

Borba, M. and Borba, C. (1982) *Self Esteem: Vol. II. More Ways to Help Children Like Themselves*, San Francisco: Harper.

Canfield, J. and Wells, H.C. (1976) *100 Ways to Enhance Self-concept in the Classroom*, Englewood Cliffs, NJ: Prentice Hall.

Ruel, N. (1989) *Sharp Eye Materials 'Me and Myself'*. Aylesbury: Ginn.

5

'She'll have a go at anything': Towards an equal opportunities policy

Janice Adams

each institution should have:
(a) a policy outlining aims and objectives based on a clearly articulated philosophy shared by educators and parents. This should incorporate:
(b) a policy on equal opportunities for children and adults, encompassing sex, race, class and disability, which promotes an understanding of cultural and physical diversity and challenges stereotypes, and which is responsive to local needs ...

(DES 1990: 35)

Have you glanced through the appointments pages of a newspaper recently? If so, you will probably have noticed references to equal opportunities in some of the advertisements, ranging from confident statements that 'this authority is an equal opportunities employer', to ideas about 'working towards', 'promoting' or being 'committed to' equal opportunities. But what does this actually mean in practice, and why should this be an issue of concern for those of us who work with young children? In order to begin to answer these questions, we need to consider the ways in which inequalities in society affect children's lives, to remember that 'there are groups of children who are being systematically disadvantaged because of their classification as female, black or working-class, or a combination of these categories' (David, 1990: 59).

Children's attitudes and expectations are influenced by their experiences – at home, in their communities, at nursery, playgroup or school. They receive powerful, and sometimes conflicting, messages about 'appropriate' behaviour. For example:

> The tendency for young girls to have limited expectations of the roles females can play has . . . been documented by people working in nurseries. It has been attributed to the images that they see in society at large, as well as to the way they are personally treated.
>
> (Browne and France 1986: 126)

This points to a need to respond to the Rumbold Committee's recommendation that early years educators adopt practices which offer alternatives to stereotypes of gender, race, class and disability, and which promote 'an understanding of cultural and physical diversity'. The case study which follows describes how the staff in one nursery began the process of developing an equal opportunities policy. The study also explores ways in which staff and parents can begin to work together to put the policy into practice. The setting is a large nursery centre in Stockport which caters for children between the ages of three and five, mainly on a part-time basis, for two or three days each week. However, some full-time 'extended day' and 'extended year' places are also available. The centre can cater for up to 100 children at any one time, and has a staff of 12 educarers and three teachers. (The title 'educarer', discussed in Chapter 9, has recently been introduced in place of the title of 'nursery officer', in order to reflect and recognize the important roles which staff play as both 'educators' and 'carers' of children in the centre.) Four staff make up the management team: a headteacher, deputy headteacher, deputy head of care and senior educarer. Each member of staff (apart from the headteacher) has responsibility for a group of children, and has a 'home base' within the nursery. The children join their groups on arrival and spend the first part of each session in their home base. They are then free to choose from activities throughout the nursery. The account which follows is based on data drawn from interviews with staff and parents. Additional information was gathered from policy documentation and from general observations.

First steps

Interviews with the staff revealed that the equal opportunities policy had been developed through a process of discussion and consultation involving the whole team. The headteacher described the early stages of the process as follows:

> Before we could get anything written down we had to get together in small groups and talk about what we felt equal opportunities was all about . . . We teased out and discussed lots of different issues . . . and then we began to break them down, when staff became a little more confident about discussion. We also went on any in-service training courses that we could, any documents and articles that I could find I brought in for staff to read – and slowly it evolved . . .

The headteacher also discussed the effect of bringing in new resources (books, puzzles, posters and so on), which involved the staff in discussion about images and stereotypes, and contributed to raising awareness of equal opportunities issues. Other significant factors emerged from interviews with the educarers. They described their role in the process:

> We always go about things in the same way on a new policy. We have team meetings – we brainstorm, and senior managers sit in with us, and we all brainstorm ideas that we think should go into the policy. The whole team will do this, so we can hopefully get different ideas from all of us – you might have forgotten something, but someone else is going to remember – and then it's brought to a staff meeting and everyone discusses it.

In this nursery, the process of policy development is enhanced by the existence of well-established procedures for consultation. The organization of small discussion groups in the early stages, and the support of senior managers, increased the opportunities for all staff to contribute their ideas. The above comments also seem to suggest that the staff have a positive attitude towards sharing different ideas and experiences.

It was also evident from the interviews that a considerable amount of time had been invested in the development of the equal opportunities policy. The 'brainstorming' sessions involved two meetings for each group, spread over a two-week period. Senior managers then produced an initial draft statement, based on the ideas of the whole team. The headteacher described the next stage of the process:

> We brought the draft to the staff meeting, with a copy for everyone, and we went through every bit of it, talking . . . Now that took about three staff meetings to get through it all, and as we were going through we were deciding as a staff what we felt was right for us, and bits that maybe we weren't ready to address, and then we formulated our draft policy, and then brought it back to the staff again – everyone seemed quite happy with it at the time.

This indicates a continued commitment to consultation, in order to reach a consensus which all staff could support. This increases the likelihood of staff having 'ownership' of the policy, which is essential if the policy is to succeed in practice. This is in line with the findings of other studies of the process of policy development. For example, Epstein and Sealey (1990) suggest that the involvement of all staff in policy development is essential if a coherent approach is to be achieved, and point out that the process of constructing a policy is an educative experience for the staff because it raises awareness of the underlying issues. These views are echoed by Leicester (1989: 59), who sees the advantages of a whole-school approach to policy development as including:

> encouragement, support, justification and guidance for worth-while developments in the school. A further important advantage lies in the process of constructing such a policy. It is important that all the staff of the school are involved, so that they will feel able to 'own' the policy, and also because the process is itself a learning one.

To summarize, the process of policy development in this nursery involved:

- discussion and consultation;
- in-service training;
- access to information about equal opportunities;
- support from senior managers;
- positive staff attitudes;

- a whole-team approach;
- investment in resources;
- creating time for debate and discussion.

The process described above began over three years ago, shortly after the appointment of the headteacher. Parents were not actively involved in the early stages of policy development because the head felt that the staff needed time to gain confidence, and to clarify their own thinking, before extending the discussion to other parties. In the three years since then, a commitment to working in partnership with parents has been a priority within the nursery, and recent policy initiatives have included parents from the outset.

Aims and principles

The policy statement drawn up by the staff outlines their aims and organization, and addresses the issues of partnership and resources.
An analysis of this policy statement suggests that the key areas of concern are:

- a commitment to giving all children access to a wide range of experiences;
- enabling children to make choices without bias and stereotyping;
- a commitment to combating discrimination and stereotyping;
- developing a context in which all children feel valued;
- fostering attitudes of tolerance and understanding of others;
- encouraging co-operation rather than competition.

These aims commit the staff to working towards a quality learning environment for young children, which is in line with recommendations of the Rumbold Committee (DES 1990) and also of HMI:

> the curriculum for young children needs to be broad, balanced, differentiated and relevant; to take into account the assessment of children's progress; to promote equal opportunities irrespective of gender, ethnic grouping or socioeconomic background; and to respond effectively to children's special educational needs.
>
> (DES 1989b: 9)

AIMS

As educators at Hollywood Park we are committed to meeting the needs of the whole child; to prepare children for life in society today and for their future. Our aims and objectives are related to the cognitive, social, emotional and physical needs of each child to enable them to experience a wide and balanced curriculum in the nursery.

We aim to welcome all children and help them reach their potential. To enable children to make choices without bias or stereotyping. To affirm each child's sense of values and self-worth. To help each child towards understanding the values and self-worth of others. To encourage cooperation rather than competition.

ORGANISATION

The organisation and management of the centre reflects the commitment of all staff to communicate and implement a policy of equal opportunities for all children.

No child will be excluded from experiencing any type of activity; staff plan for and monitor play to ensure that each child has optimum access. Solitary play, play alongside others, co-operative play, and group work are settings in which each child will be encouraged to learn.

The staff at the centre have all participated in equal opportunities training, and are developing strategies for combating discrimination and stereotyping, and are working towards developing learning materials that promote awareness, understanding and tolerance.

Communicating this policy involves an awareness of the language we use, a respect for other languages, customs, and differing abilities. Several staff at the centre are learning the British Sign Language. Books, posters and notices in the centre will reflect these commitments.

PARTNERSHIP

Working in partnership with parents and carers. An explanation of our policy is discussed with new parents. We show examples of current children's work, resources, welcome notices in many languages, and photographs of children working together, to all new parents and interested visitors. Beginning a dialogue: what are we offering your child? – setting goals together, and establishing support and involvement. We invite parents and members of the community to the centre, such as a postwoman, a male nurse, to work alongside us and provide opportunities for learning which counter stereotypes.

RESOURCES

Promoting positive images. Learning with materials that reflect the diversity of cultures, gender roles, and disabilities – for example, musical instruments from around the world, jig-saw puzzles which show boys as caring and girls as active, and books that portray disabled children as central characters.

We check existing resources for bias or stereotyping, work sensitively with resources, and continue to monitor and evaluate resources.

Our equal opportunities resource base has been set up to enable us all to work together to meet our aims – the equipment may be borrowed by parents and carers for their child to use together at home; staff working with the children at the centre will use the room for group work and borrow equipment to use with children in their own rooms: the room will also be used as a reference and information base for other early years educators.

From policy to practice

Strategies for providing choice and access

The policy statement identifies the importance of planning and monitoring 'to ensure that each child has optimum access'. The headteacher also commented that activities would be modified if necessary, to ensure that all children could participate:

> Children with special needs are valued and involved in everything that's going on in the centre, and if there's a problem with it, then we make it right so that so they can get involved and join in with the rest of the children.

A further strategy discussed during interview was that of positive discrimination, for example:

for girls to use the woodwork and gain the skills that they require to then join in a mixed-sex group ... the same with boys in the house area – they get an opportunity to go into the house and play there without girls saying 'you've got to be daddy'.

Strategies for challenging stereotypes

The headteacher and educarers commented on the importance of selecting and monitoring resources in order to eliminate bias and promote positive images. This is confirmed in the policy statement, which outlines a commitment to:

Learning with materials that reflect the diversity of cultures, gender roles, and disabilities – for example, musical instruments from around the world, jig-saw puzzles which show boys as caring and girls as active, and books that portray disabled children as central characters.

Many of these resources have been gathered into an 'equal opportunities resource base' which is used by parents, children and staff. Materials from the base can be borrowed by parents to use at home.

Other strategies include providing role models for the children – inviting a male nurse to the nursery, for example. Staff also aim to be aware of the language they use, avoiding sexist comments about 'strong boys' and 'pretty girls', for example.

Strategies for influencing attitudes and values

This is a more difficult area to quantify. The strategies which are used to challenge stereotypes also have a role to play in influencing attitudes: the selection of resources will affect the messages which children receive about different cultural traditions, for example. The nursery environment is therefore seen as important, but the policy statement also recognizes the importance of staff attitudes:

Communicating this policy involves an awareness of the language we use, a respect for other languages, customs, and differing abilities. Several staff at the centre are learning the British Sign Language. Books, posters and notices in the centre will reflect these commitments.

The headteacher and educarers stressed the importance of staff monitoring their own practice and considering the messages which they might be communicating through their words and actions. They all agreed that this can be difficult in practice. The head-teacher commented that 'staff are much more aware now – they are working on it. But you can easily slip back into the ways of working that are traditional to you.' This was echoed by one of the educarers: 'it's being aware of your own practice – sometimes it's hard trying to think about what you're doing and saying'.

From my observations of the staff, it was apparent that they often used resources to initiate discussions about 'race' or 'gender'. This might involve challenging stereotypes – for example, the story *My Dad Takes Care of Me* (Quinlan 1990) provided opportunities for talking about men in caring roles. Using resources in this way would seem to be a crucial factor in the success of an equal opportunities initiative. Epstein and Sealey (1990: 50) comment that:

> while resources are essential to the development of new curriculum initiatives, they cannot in themselves teach the pupils. The teacher has to understand thoroughly not only the resources, but the principles behind the development of the curriculum.

This was an issue of concern to the nursery headteacher, particularly in relation to the use of the equal opportunities resource base. She spoke of her intention to develop support materials to accompany the resources, and increase awareness and understanding of their intended purpose – for example, cards which provide ideas for the use of the equipment, including vocabulary and language:

> That would be a wonderful resource – a student, or a parent coming in would be able to look at the card, and look at the language to use, and would feel more confident about using the equipment.

This is a particularly important consideration in relation to representations of 'race' and 'culture'. If resources are used in ways which emphasize the 'exotic' aspects of different cultures, there is a danger that stereotypes will be reinforced, rather than challenged. One of the educarers commented that she tried to avoid this by using a mixture of resources:

> Books with black characters will show many different situations – people doing everyday things, going to school . . . Sometimes they might show Asian characters in saris, but not all the time . . . The activity this morning, with the books and puppets was like that – just a family going to the park . . .

This presents a view of cultural diversity which moves beyond stereotypes or tokenism.

The equal opportunities policy permeates all aspects of nursery practice, including planning and monitoring, organization, and selection of resources. But the key to the successful implementation of policy is the commitment and awareness of the staff, and the quality of their interactions with the children.

Sharing policy aims with parents

The Rumbold Committee (DES 1990: 35) recommends that policies should be based on 'a clearly articulated philosophy shared by educators and parents'. This section will consider parents views about equal opportunities, and describe how the nursery staff tried to share their concerns with parents.

Parents' views of involvement

> Here you're more than welcome to come in – some mornings I don't leave till half nine. It's somewhere you feel comfortable and the children pick up on that, too.

> They don't talk down to you here if you're a single parent, which other places do.

Positive feelings about the nursery were evident during all of the interviews. Parents talked of feeling 'welcome', 'comfortable' and 'involved', but not pressurized:

> You can be as involved as you want to be here – if you're too busy or anything they don't mind. You can help as much as you want to.

Several parents commented on the value of events such as discos and barbeques where staff and parents could socialize. These seemed to contribute to the process of developing relationships and helping parents to feel involved with the nursery. Parents also commented on the value of newsletters and meetings, and felt that they were kept informed about things which were happening in the nursery. These could also be a way of challenging stereotypes:

> It's the way things are worded, because where we used to go to the mother and toddler group, it's now a parent and toddler group. I think dads would feel put off if they saw 'mums' and toddlers, they'd feel excluded . . . And I've noticed in the newsletters as well articles that involve dads.

Parents views of the equal opportunities policy

> You can tell as soon as you walk through the door.

> You're really well aware of it.

Most parents were aware that the nursery had an equal opportunities policy. They found out about this by talking with staff, attending meetings, or reading information on notice boards. Not all parents were sure about the aims of the policy, however, even though the policy statement was on display in the nursery. Time seemed to be a factor in this, with several parents commenting that they often had to 'rush in and out' when bringing or collecting their children, so that they could not always stop to read material on display. They did respond to the visual images around the nursery, however, mentioning displays related to events such as the Chinese new year. One parent commented that:

> You're not struck by white middle-class images when you walk into the building.

while another said:

> I've noticed like at Christmas, instead of having the snow-man, it was the snow-woman.

The nursery environment clearly made an impact, and helped to communicate the commitment to equal opportunities. Parents were generally supportive, and felt that it was good for children to learn about 'other cultures', for example. Yet some parents remained unsure about the process of monitoring resources for bias or stereotyping:

> I've come in and watched them doing jigsaws but I've not really looked at the pictures or took it in.

> I don't really think about it – I just let the children choose what they like.

Opportunities for discussing these issues with the staff could, however, make a difference to levels of awareness, though:

> We were talking about . . . one particular toy, and the box didn't have girls on, or it didn't have black people on, and they wanted it to, say, have girls on . . . which seems right, but it just seemed normal to me, it's the norm that you keep seeing all the time, but they'd spotted something that *should* be there. I thought that was really good.

Parents' views of stereotyping

> Jamie loves to borrow Lucy's pram, and he gets the cups and saucers out, but he also loves doing everything the lads do.

Many comments similar to this were made by parents during interviews. They referred to their children choosing and enjoying activities which were not typically associated with their sex. Yet there was a clear demarcation along gender lines – *he* would play with *her* dolls or cooker, or *she* would play with *his* Lego or cars. One parent commented that her son, an only child, only had 'boys' toys' at home, but:

Parent: When he goes to see my sister, she's got four girls, so he's got no choice but to play with the prams and dolls because she hasn't got anything for a boy.
Interviewer: Would you buy him anything like that?
Parent: No . . . I wouldn't think so, no.
Interviewer: Why?
Parent: Basically, I never really think about it, I mean, they've got a mind of their own eventually,

> haven't they, and when they go to school they
> get segregated anyway.

This parent seemed to feel that different sex roles were almost inevitable, and so there was little point in intervening. Comments made by other parents, though, suggested that they felt that gender roles were constructed out of children's experiences:

> I must admit to treating them [his son and daughter] a bit differently, if I'm honest.

> When you go buying things, you automatically think, oh I'll get a pram for her – I think you automatically do it even if you don't intend to. You see, they see other girls playing with them, and want it for themselves . . . I think you'd have to live in a little house on your own to get them not to do it, where they'd see nobody else.

Most parents seemed to take the view that it is very difficult to bring about change, even though they expressed support for what the nursery was trying to achieve:

> It's what the media portrays, isn't it, you can't change what is happening all around you.

> I agree fully with equal opportunities all across the board, but it's been split for hundreds of years – you've got a long way to go.

There were some notes of optimism, however, with several parents commenting on changes since they were at school, for example in relation to subject choice, and they were pleased that their children would have access to a wide range of experiences:

> She'll have a go at anything, like computers and things as well, whereas years ago you'd have thought, no it's just for boys, you know, it's too technical. But now they're saying, well it's fine if you want to do that . . . so then they'll be more inclined when they leave school. Then they can do what they want to.

It seemed that many parents believed that sex roles are 'created' not 'given', and can be influenced by experience. The main difference between their views and nursery policy is that they feel less confident about bringing about change, particularly when the reality of their own lives reflects traditional gender divisions:

> I make the tea, he washes up. I do the ironing, he's always under the car. I clean the windows . . . that's how it is for me.

Parents' views of nursery organization

> They try to do all sorts for the children – you come in in the morning, and there's all kinds set out. They're all good things, every day.

> Here she can use whatever she wants, as and when she wants . . . it's not just the girls playing with the dolls and the boys with the trucks.

Most parents seemed to be familiar with the organization of the nursery. They could see the activities on offer when they brought children to the nursery, and knew what their children had been doing from talking to the staff and from things which the children took home.

One feature of the nursery's equal opportunities policy which was identified by all of the parents, was that all of the children were encouraged to participate in all activities. This strategy was regarded positively, because the children were felt to be 'learning' and 'gaining confidence'. So, although parents did not always take active steps to challenge stereotypes when choosing toys for their children to play with at home, they valued the fact that their children could have access to a wide range of activities at the nursery.

Some parents also saw a link between the day-to-day organisation and the general ethos of the nursery:

> It's a learning by experience thing here – there's no pressure, they're still letting them be children, but they're making them aware that there's always two sides to everything. This is the age when you need everybody to understand that everybody's equal.

> They're allowed to make choices, so it's not about putting someone in pigeonholes, being forced to take on a certain role.

This corresponds very closely with the aim of the nursery to enable children to make choices without bias or stereotyping.

In this nursery, then, it seems that:

• parents have access to information about the equal opportunities policy from several sources, including meetings, informal discussions with staff, written information, displays and notices;
• parents were supportive of nursery policy, but were not always aware of specific aims or strategies;
• parents valued the learning opportunities which the nursery offered to their children;
• parents expressed varying degrees of concern about issues such as stereotyping.

What does this case study illustrate about the process of sharing policy aims with parents, as recommended by the Rumbold Committee? What do educators need to consider if they are to achieve the goal of developing policies based on shared principles and philosophies? Two issues which seem to me to be particularly important are the quality of *relationships* and the effectiveness of *communication*.

Developing effective relationships

The basis of relationships between educators and parents or carers is all too often a hierarchical one, with the staff as 'experts' who control the way in which parents are enabled to participate in the life of the school or nursery. Within this framework, parents are encouraged to 'help' in school, provide practical support in the form of fund-raising, and so on, but are offered little possibility of being given a voice in relation to policy.

Eisenstadt (1986) is critical of nurseries which seek to involve parents in order to 'improve' their parenting skills. She argues instead for a 'partnership' model of involvement, which responds to parents' own perceptions of their needs, and treats individuals as competent and capable. This approach is also advocated by Pugh and De'Ath (1989: 330), who define 'partnership' as 'a working relationship that is characterised by a sense of shared purpose, mutual respect, and the willingness to negotiate. This implies a sharing of information, responsibility, skills, decision-making and accountability.' In the case study, a sense of mutual respect was evident from the way parents talked about the nursery. They felt comfortable, and were not 'talked down to', which made it easier for them to express their own concerns. This indicates that the nursery was laying the foundations from which 'partnership' can be developed.

Fathers and male carers were also made to feel welcome, and were encouraged to become involved in the nursery. David (1990: 38) argues that for many practitioners the term 'parent' actually means 'mother', and that many models of parental involvement are based around a traditional view of women's role as 'mother and primary family carer, at home'. Thus, mothers are assumed to be available to 'help' in school, or with outings.

This view of women as prime carers of children is frequently reinforced by the nature of parental involvement in many schools. Edwards and Redfern (1988) comment that 'an objective look at who actually comes to help in school hours reveals that it is mostly women – mothers, grandmothers, big sisters' (1988: 158) and that many of the jobs which they are asked to do, 'preparation, washing, cooking, sewing – fit all too neatly into the stereotypical role of women' (1988: 118). This suggests that strategies for involving parents need to be monitored and reviewed in order to avoid perpetuating stereotypes.

Staff attitudes clearly have an important effect on the quality of relationships. Are parents welcomed and accepted, or judged and made to feel inadequate? How 'open' is the school or nursery? How do parents gain access? Atkin *et al.* (1988: 46) found that few schools are actually 'as open to parents as they think they are, or would like to be! For, in spite of parents' apparent familiarity with their children's schools and teachers, access was both conditional and limited'. The research of Atkin *et al.* suggests that even parents who have gone through the process of becoming 'familiar' with a school did not necessarily have a clear understanding of the aims of the school: 'the evidence of one's eyes is not always easy to interpret . . . being knowledgeable about something is not necessarily the same as understanding what is going on, and making a critical evaluation of it'.

The research also found that parents were frequently familiar with school routines and individual members of staff, but were less likely to be familiar with the detail of school policies. Similar points are evident from the comments of parents in this case study, who were aware of daily routines, and on good terms with the staff, but were unsure about specific policy aims. The process of 'becoming familiar' is an important step on the way to closer collaboration, though, because 'closer contact and involvement with schools led many [parents] to identify more with the school's goals and activities' (Atkin *et al.* 1988: 83).

Towards effective communication

Once parents have become 'familiar' with a school or nursery, how can information be shared so that parents have a clearer picture of what takes place each day? The case study illustrates some possibilities: making documentation available, producing newsletters, making use of display areas and notice boards. But the most effective communication occurs when staff and parents can spend time talking to each other about issues of concern. This can lead to increased understanding, as in the example of a parent talking with staff about stereotypes on toy packages. In this case, the parent was very positive about what the staff were saying – 'it just seemed normal to me . . . but they'd spotted something that *should* be there. I thought that was really good' – and an opportunity had arisen to talk about policy aims in some depth.

But with an area as complex as equal opportunities, parents and staff may not always be in agreement. What happens, for example, if a father insists that he does not want his son to play with dolls, or parents express concern about children learning about different faiths and cultures? If parents are made to feel uncomfortable about their own lifestyles and roles, then it is difficult for home and school to work in partnership. But if stereotypes are never questioned or challenged, alternatives cannot be offered or explored. Kelly (1989: 103) has commented that the 'right to intervene' rests on being able to convince others that ideas are valuable and in the best interests of the children. This seemed to be the basis of the good relationships illustrated by the case study. The parents valued the experiences which were offered to their children, and felt that the staff had their children's 'best interests' at heart. This creates a context in which ideas can be exchanged and discussed. Wolfendale (1992: 95) argues that it is 'parents' *right* to be party to contemporary thinking about equal opportunities' and that:

if those of us in education are going to take our responsibilities for creating quality education seriously, we can proceed no further, in this newer climate of accountability and quality assurance procedures, without the equal participation of informed parents who understand the philosophy as well as the practice.

Concluding thoughts

Developing an equal opportunities policy is a complex and challenging task, which requires commitment and enthusiasm. There are no short cuts, and success depends on staff and parents becoming convinced of the *need* to adopt anti-discriminatory practices. As the nursery headteacher observed:

It's a case of us coming to terms with the fact that this is a very slow process, and we've got to keep working at it – we may not see any signs displayed that we are getting very far, then all of a sudden we'll see something, and it makes it all worthwhile.

The quality of experience which children can have when their educators adopt an equal opportunities policy is captured vividly in the words of one of the nursery parents:

I don't know if the next school will have this type of attitude towards things, but once she's experienced it here, I think it will stay, regardless of where she's going, or what people say. She'll have an opinion, and an outlook and an attitude which will be *hers*. She can be whatever she wants to be. No one will be able to change that.

Some questions to consider ...

... when developing policy

- Who will be involved?
- How much time is available for meetings and discussions?
- Do you need further information and resources?
- Who will take responsibility for gathering information?
- What are your main aims and concerns, and why?

- What has already been achieved?
- What are your priorities for development?

... when working with parents and carers

- Are parents made welcome in your workplace?
- How much contact is there between staff and parents?
- Could this be extended?
- How do parents gain information?
- Are they consulted about new developments?
- Are there opportunities for sharing ideas about aims and policies?
- How can you make time for this?

... concerning partnership

- The Rumbold Report and many others use 'partnership' to describe the ideal relationship with parents. Is that an accurate description or are you striving for some other sort of relationship?

Suggested further reading

Browne, N. and France, P. (1986) *Untying The Apron Strings*. Milton Keynes: Open University Press.
Epstein, Debbie and Sealey, Alison (1990) *Where It Really Matters ... Developing Anti-racist Education in Predominantly White Primary Schools*. Birmingham: Development Education Centre.
Wolfendale, Sheila (1992) *Empowering Parents and Teachers: Working for Children*. London: Cassell.

6

'We only speak English here, don't we?': Supporting language development in a multilingual context

Caroline Barratt-Pugh

> Most children will be adept speakers and listeners by the time
> they enter pre-school provision. . . . Some children will be
> competent speakers of a language other than English and
> they will need skilful help to master English while retaining
> their mother tongue language.
>
> (DES 1990: 40)

On first reading, this statement appears to be fairly straightfor-
ward and reflects what many early years workers would consider
to be common sense. For decades early years theory and practice
have to a large extent been based on the view that carers should
'build on what children know', and 'start where children are at'.
This 'child-centred' approach to education is seen as the basis for
quality and equality in the early years. In this chapter I will argue
that, despite the best intentions, for many children and particularly bilingual and multilingual children the opposite is true. That
is, the way in which education and care are constructed can actually deny and/or displace the experiences and understandings some
children bring to school.

Rabina is the central character in my story. I start by identifying the diversity of language skills that Rabina is developing in
her home and community. Next, I follow Rabina to school and

explore the ways in which the interactions that Rabina is involved in contribute to her emerging linguistic competence. I then go on to identify several issues which emerge from the analysis of these interactions and conclude by raising a number of questions about current practice in relation to the provision of quality and equality.

Rabina is five years old and has lived in the North of England for a year. She arrived from Punjab in Pakistan, with her mother and younger brother (Imran) to join her father and older sister (Nasreen). The whole family moved into a terrace house in a community made up of mainly Punjabi-speaking families, with a few monolingual English-speaking families who have lived in the area for generations.

Identifying communicative competence in the home and community

It is 11.30 on a cold but bright September morning. Rabina is sitting with her mother, next-door neighbour and older sister, looking curiously at the 'lady' who has just been invited in. The 'lady' keeps gesturing towards Rabina and smiling, she has brought some books and gives them to Rabina. Rabina moves rapidly away from the books and the 'lady'. Her mother says something in Punjabi and Rabina picks the books up. In between the 'lady' speaking in English, Nasreen translating into Punjabi and her mother replying, Rabina combines her knowledge of Punjabi with a few English words that she recognizes and begins to piece the puzzle together. This is her new teacher.

If we step back and take a brief look at other events that Rabina is involved in during the day, we find a number of equally complex meanings being constructed through a variety of linguistic inter-actions. In the morning Rabina has been using Mirpuri Punjabi (a regional dialect) to play with Imran, argue with Nasreen and ask her parents if she can go to her friend's birthday party. In addition to this, she has been trying to make sense of a variety of English dialects while watching television. After lunch Rabina will go to the corner shop and use a Yorkshire dialect of English to buy some sweets and milk. If she meets friends on the way she may switch between English and Punjabi depending upon the shared language and the context of their talk. Later on in the afternoon she will go to the mosque to study the Koran in Arabic. Finally, before going to bed Nasreen might tell her a story written in Urdu. Nasreen is learning Urdu at the community school, as Urdu is the language of the wider community and Rabina will probably join Nasreen next year.

Even from this brief snapshot, it would appear that Rabina knows a great deal about language and how it works. She has begun to understand:

* *That different contexts demand different linguistic systems.* Already Rabina is able to assess the situation and select the appropriate language. In addition to this, she is able to judge when it is necessary to combine and switch languages.
* *That language can be used for a number of different purposes.* Evidence suggests that Rabina is able to choose the appropriate form of language from her developing repertoire. In just one day Rabina has used language to argue, to negotiate, to ask for permission, to recite and learn religious text, to purchase goods and to enter into a world of fantasy.
* *That language defines and maintains social relationships.* Through observation of, and involvement in, a variety of contexts Rabina is beginning to recognize that the style and form of interaction changes according to the situation. For example, it is clear that the way in which Nasreen talks to the teacher is quite different to the way in which she talks to her mother.
* *That culture is embedded in, transmitted through and changed by language.* Rabina's interactions reflect the internalization of the complex conventions of particular cultural and religious 'norms'. Rabina is striving to make sense of the immediate culture of her family and community as well as the wider culture which permeates her everyday.
* *That language shapes and mediates identity.* Although we can only speculate at this point, it is worth asking to what extent Rabina's developing sense of self worth is being challenged or confirmed as she moves through the day. For example, in the events out-lined above Rabina has been constructed as a language user in several different ways: as a competent Mirpuri Punjabi speaker (by her family); as a non-English speaker (by the teacher); as a bilingual Punjabi and English speaker (by her peers); as a reciter of Arabic (by her religious instructor); as a learner of a 'new

language' (by her older sister). Each construction will to some extent influence the way in which Rabina 'sees' herself and the way in which she responds in each context.

- *That one language can be translated into another in order to create shared understanding.* Rabina is beginning to understand that similar meanings can be expressed in different languages, yet some things appear to be harder to explain in one language than another. This may lead her to recognize that different languages construct the world differently, giving bilingual speakers potential access to a multiplicity of meanings.
- *That English is the dominant language of the wider society.* Rabina has soon recognized that not everybody shares her linguistic competence and that in some contexts it is her responsibility to learn and use English in order to communicate.
- *That reading and writing are 'done' in specific contexts for particular purposes.* Rabina's involvement in particular cultural and religious literacy practices, such as reciting the Koran, is shaping her understanding of what counts as literacy and how literacy is 'done'.

Rabina is involved in making choices about the appropriate type and form of language and appears to be successfully operating in a number of different languages. She uses language in a way that enables her to understand and create complex and new meanings in order to take part in and be part of a range of cultural and social contexts. At this point in time it would seem that language is, as Breen (1993) suggested, Rabina's most 'powerful asset'.

As we follow Rabina into her first term in school, to what extent will she be able to capitalize on this wealth of communicative competence?

Exploring aspects of communication in the classroom

The Rumbold Report (DES 1990) clearly states that provision should be made to enable bilingual children to *retain* their mother tongue. But is this really enough in the light of the complex range of understandings Rabina has demonstrated? In order to tap into Rabina's creativity there is a need to design a context in which Rabina can *build on* and *extend* all of her communicative powers, which clearly go beyond the sum of their parts. But how possible is this within the constraints of the current educational and political climate?

It is 8.45 on a mild but wet September morning. Rabina is sitting on the carpet in the book corner looking anxious yet excited. She recognizes the teacher as she comes into the classroom. Rabina has just left her younger brother crying in the nursery with her mother who is trying to reassure him. Nasreen is on her way to the new middle school with her friends. It is the first day of the new term. During his first day at the nursery Imran found that he could not understand anyone and no one could understand him. He wanted to go home.

During her first day at school Rabina found that it was okay to use Punjabi in certain situations, but that some children did not like to and did not like you to. In addition to this, teachers could not understand you and you could not understand them. She wanted to go home.

During her first day at middle school Nasreen found that much of what she had learned at first school did not really count here and that English was the language that was preferred. She wanted to go home.

First days are notoriously traumatic for many children and teachers/carers, and I will return to this important issue later. Meanwhile, the following descriptions give us a snapshot of some of the events Rabina was involved in during her first few weeks at school. Although brief and therefore limited, they do raise a number of general issues in relation to quality and equality for bilingual children.

News-time

The children are sitting on the carpet in front of the teacher, the register has been taken and the teacher has asked children to put up their hand if they have some news about the weekend. Rabina is sitting at the front, watching the other children. She doesn't put her hand up, as yet perhaps she is not sure what counts as news or the procedure that is involved.

The teacher chooses six children who stand next to her in a row waiting for their turn. As the children tell their news the teacher puts their name on the board and writes some 'key words'. Abdul has been chosen. He appears to be very keen and excited, whispering to another child and trying to move to the front of the queue. Eventually it is his turn.

Abdul: Good morning, everybody.
Children: Good morning, Abdul.
Teacher: Stand up straight, Abdul, right.
Abdul: Um ... er you know last night um when it were um
             dark ... um in the night time. Well, these boys ...
             men um we don't know ... these men came and
             and ... er put brick in window and um ... police-
             man came and they don't know um say we don't
             know and
Teacher: Slowly, Abdul ...
Abdul: Yes, and and my mum cry, my dad shouting ...
Teacher: Oh dear, I am sorry, that's terrible, are you all right?
             ... I hope the police catch them. Now have you
             anything nice to tell us?

Creative art

Rabina is standing with an apron on around a table covered in a plastic sheet. There are a variety of crayons in the middle of the table and some large sheets of paper. The children have been asked to draw a picture of themselves to go on the 'Our Class' wall. There are a number of small hand mirrors on the table for the children to look closely at themselves. Rabina draws herself in a shalwar kameez and, on looking at Yasmin, is quietly urged to use the pink crayon for her skin colour. Both girls giggle as they give themselves bright red cheeks.

Cooking

As part of the topic on 'food' the class have been making a variety of dishes and writing the recipes in the appropriate language. They have made vegetable soup, Chinese stir fry, and today they are making vegetable curry. Noreen's mum has come in to help. During the process some of the children begin to complain and make negative comments about the food, half laughing, half embarrassed – 'I'm not eating Paki food'; 'It smells'; 'I'm not eating that, it makes me sick'. All eyes are on the teacher, waiting for her response.

Structured play

Noreen, Asif, and Rabina are playing in the 'post office'. The area is full of a variety of post office equipment, writing implements, stationery, booklets and information packs in a number of local languages. Rabina and Noreen appear to be making marks, that seem to resemble Arabic script, on a number of envelopes. Asif joins the group and after some exchanges in Punjabi they begin to laugh and exchange envelopes. At this point Abdul, who had been watching them, became very agitated and shouted to the teacher 'Ay, we only speak English here, don't we?' After a very heated exchange between Abdul and Asif in English, Rabina left the post office and did not speak to anyone for the remaining half hour before lunch.

Story-time

The children have read the story of *The Paper Bag Princess* (Munsch 1982) with the teacher, and as part of a drama lesson are going to work in groups to prepare a party to celebrate Princess Elizabeth's bravery. Each group has been asked to take one aspect of the party and then present their ideas to the princess. There are four areas to be worked on: catering, costumes, decorations and entertainment.

At the end of the week each group is ready to present their ideas to 'Princess Elizabeth'. The teacher begins by asking who would like to be the princess. Several hands including Rabina's, shoot up eagerly. The teacher continues: 'Now what would the princess look like?' As the children build up a picture of a white Anglo-Saxon girl, with blue eyes and long blond hair, Rabina slowly puts her hand down. The teacher questions this portrayal and suggests that there are all sorts of princesses, referring the children to their knowledge of 'real' princesses.

Parents' day

It is the end of the first term. Parents have been invited to the school to talk informally to the teachers and look at the children's work. Rabina's portfolio of work includes a number of writing and drawing samples clearly indicating the progress she has been making. There will be food and some singing in the hall. Rabina's mum is coming and Rabina has asked her not to wear a sari. Rabina whispers to her mum while showing her some of her work but seems reluctant to talk. By the end of the evening there is an air of frustration between Rabina and her mum and they leave before the singing has started.

These events represent a 'snapshot' taken from a whole range of experiences that Rabina was involved in during her first term at school. While recognizing the limitations of such descriptions and the numerous interpretations that could be applied, I wish to discuss a number of general issues that these 'events' raise for me. These will be considered under three main headings.

Examining the link between home and school

The transition from home to nursery, from nursery to school and from school to school has been identified as a potentially traumatic experience for all children (this is addressed more fully in Chapter 7). In relation to Rabina's family, the transition for all three children appeared to be particularly difficult. They were not just traversing physical and emotional worlds but stepping, within a few streets, from culture to culture, into an almost wholly English-speaking environment. Clearly, for children who do not speak the dominant language or share the dominant 'norms' and expectations the problems may be magnified. However, the notion of a shared language and culture is not the only aspect of transition that needs to be considered.

With the advent of devolution, a number of brochures and booklets are being produced by schools. These are used as a means of introducing parents and children to the school, with the aim of helping them to understand what school is all about. Very often there are sections which describe what children should be able to do before they come to school and how parents/carers can help their child to cope with the demands of school, particularly in relation to reading and writing.

Clearly contact between home and school is seen as a way of easing the transition and promoting positive relationships. However, in striving to inform and involve parents, to what extent is a notion of 'uniformity' being constructed and difference being denied? What images of 'childhood' and 'good parenting' are being presented? Are schools painting, and even demanding, a particular kind of 'good child' and 'good parent'? If parents and children don't 'fit' the 'description', is their culture, their language, their very 'being' seen as problematic? Do the demands placed on parents in relation to what children should be able to do, and how parents should interact with children, take account of cultural differences? Are parents in fact being instructed on how to do the work of schools, and could this be seen as 'parenting the parents'? Finally, in relation to Rabina, would her communicative competence be seen as inadequate, even before she starts school, bringing into question the whole notion of quality and equality?

Building on and extending communicative competence

Children's use of and response to community languages

The school had a policy of support for the children's home languages, recognizing the importance of this at an intellectual and emotional level. On entering the school a range of languages could be heard in the playground and occasionally in the corridors. Yet it is interesting to note that many of the children seemed reluctant to use their home language in the classroom.

In Rabina's class several of the older children denied speaking their home language, and by the end of the first term Rabina seemed embarrassed when her mother spoke in Punjabi. Occasionally, an English-speaking child would laugh at children speaking Punjabi, commenting that they 'sound funny' or 'talk rubbish', and demanding that the group 'talked proper'. Perhaps the English-speaking children felt excluded or were commenting on something they could not understand. Or perhaps echoing the racism that may pervade their everyday life, in which Asian languages are often devalued and actively discouraged.

In addition to this, we may deduce from the incident in the class 'post office' that the issue is about more than making a choice between using English and a home language. Abdul is a Bengali speaker, and in this context a member of a minority within a minority. English may have been the common language and therefore Abdul's only way of gaining access to the conversation.

Alternatively, as the only Bengali speaker in the class, he may have felt a heightened sense of isolation – perhaps feeling culturally closer to or more comfortable with his Muslim peers yet unable to talk with them. Finally, he may have internalized the concept that as the dominant language, English was the only language spoken or worth speaking. Rabina's subsequent facial expression, body language and silence suggested an air of concern and/or confusion.

Clearly, the notion of mother-tongue support is an extremely complex and controversial issue which has been debated for a number of years. Perhaps now more than ever teachers/carers may find themselves in a particularly difficult situation. There seems to be a dilemma between the demands of the National Curriculum, which sees mother tongue as only important in relation to the development of English, and the rhetoric of a 'child-centred' curriculum founded on the notion of equality and quality of practice and provision. Perhaps we should start by asking what the consequences are of not supporting home languages.

Cognitive and linguistic implications of multilingualism

For Imran and children like him, who are in the early stages of establishing their first language and yet are attending a nursery in which the majority of children and adults speak another language, the consequences may be far reaching.

Research has shown that 'if children are introduced to skills and concepts in a language that they do not understand, their progress will be impeded and it may take many years to catch up' (Edwards *et al.* 1988: 80). As a result, many children may become what Baker (1988) describes as 'semi-linguals'. He claims that these children are at a significant cognitive disadvantage because neither language is sufficiently well developed to enable them to cope with the demands of the nursery or classroom.

Thus it would seem that Imran is put at a disadvantage as soon as he enters the nursery, if there is no simultaneous support for his home language. This is particularly worrying for the number of four-year-olds who are attending school full-time and perhaps involved in a more 'formal' curriculum in which English is the key means of communication and participation.

For older children the situation is equally worrying. Ray-chaudhuri (1989: 10) claims that the strong emphasis in the National

Curriculum on English will 'push the bilingual child off the edge of the British education system . . . [and in effect] set the seal on their sense of exclusion from British society'.

As well as academic consequences there are emotional and cultural consequences. Edwards *et al.* (1988: 81) argue that:

> First language maintenance . . . is . . . important in its own right as an enrichment, symbol and expression of individual and ethnic group identity and culture . . . If we devalue and ignore the first languages of linguistic minority groups we are ignoring and devaluing part of those people and their culture.

In addition to this, I would argue that if home languages are not supported, the very nature of the community may change. At one extreme the languages of minority groups in Britain may begin to disappear and in the process children may be cut off from communication with their grandparents and in some cases even their parents. At the other extreme, as communities set up their own schools, while reinforcing culture, religion and identity, this may also result in further segregation and isolation. In relation to Rabina, as is evident from the parents' evening, it may be that she has already to some extent begun to re-evaluate the worth and appropriateness of Punjabi.

Finally, it is recognized that many parents may see the primary role of education as teaching their children English. Clearly, fluency in English is crucial to gaining access to the wider society at this present time. However, evidence from around the world suggests that the dual aims of supporting home languages and developing English are not mutually exclusive. The apparent difficulty in achieving these aims seems to lie not with parents or children but with education policy and resourcing.

Exploring patterns of interaction in the classroom

Providing quality and equality through language goes beyond support for the learner's home languages. There is a need to consider the actual patterns of interaction in the nursery or classroom in order to identify ways in which Rabina's ongoing attempts to make sense of the world and create meaning, through her use of language, are recognized and extended.

We see that Rabina has the opportunity to interact in a variety of situations. Rabina is involved in one-to-one situations, in a small group and as part of the class as a whole. The activities are planned as a means of supporting children's learning through language. Language is seen as the medium through which learning takes place.

The activities in Rabina's class are based on a child-centred approach to learning in which learners are viewed as active participants. Development takes place through exploration and problem-solving, and learners self-select for activities as far as possible and have some control over the decision-making process.

Once again each of the events described above can be analysed in a variety of ways and represent only a glimpse of Rabina's experiences at school. However, from each event it is possible to raise some general issues.

Hearing everybody's story

News-time seems to be an important part of a child-centred approach and is done in a number of different ways. In Rabina's classroom the teacher claimed to use it as a means of:

• getting to know about the children's lives outside school;
• sharing events that seem important;
• ensuring both boys and girls have an opportunity to speak;
• giving children practice in addressing a large audience;
• helping children to recall, sequence, ask and answer questions;
• maintaining control.

If quality and equality of provision and practice are related to the notion of building on children's experiences then clearly news-time and other similar forms of interaction could have an important place in the curriculum. However, Abdul's news seemed to place the teacher in a difficult position. It appeared that the incident that Abdul described was motivated by racism. In this case the teacher chose to respond briefly and ask for alternative news.

This event does raise the question of acceptability and authenticity. Are some 'realities' more acceptable than others? Will some children begin to create 'news' that has much to do with procedure and conformity and less to do with meaningful interaction? If Abdul and children like him are going to be able to share experiences that are part of their everyday reality then we need to find a way of creating a context in which meaningful events, particularly those which oppress and hurt children, can be raised as part of classroom discourse.

Confronting and responding to both overt and covert racism takes many different forms depending on the context, the child and the teacher/carer. The teacher's response to racism reflects his/her attitude towards such behaviour and signals the seriousness with which such behaviour is viewed. In dealing with the children's comments about the vegetable curry, clear messages are given to the monolingual children, the children who are becoming bilingual, and the parent who is working in the classroom.

We can see how confronting racist incidents immediately, as well as incorporating anti-racist strategies into the curriculum, challenges a child-centred approach which accepts what children do and say as somehow 'natural' and therefore 'unproblematic'.

The significance of difference

The way in which Rabina responds to the teacher and her peers will be influenced by her understanding of conventions of behaviour which she has learned from interaction at home and in the community. This suggests that although culture and language are dynamic, it is important to be aware of interaction patterns and conversational conventions as well as cultural and religious 'norms' that may differ significantly from those the teacher is familiar with.

This includes knowledge about culturally based action and beliefs, as well as recognition of the values and cultural norms that are reflected through language, for example:

• body language – gestures, eye contact, holding hands, body movements;
• learning styles;
• interaction with and response to adults;
• gender- and age-related practices;
• tone, stress and intonation as indicators of meaning;
• particular speech acts – politeness, forms of address;
• markers of particular relationships – respect, deference and humility.

Clearly, for children who come from cultures in which learning is expected to be more 'ordered' and perhaps 'explicit', it could be argued that a child-centred approach actually works against them. Because they do not share the same values as the teacher and other children, they do not know what is 'important' or how to access the information they need to be successful. Once again a child-centred approach may be seen to positively disadvantage some children rather than provide equality.

Whose reality counts?

In addition to this, if literacy is seen as a socially constructed phenomenon, which children come to understand through involvement in a range of literacy practices, then Rabina already has some understanding of 'what counts' as literacy, and how literacy is 'done'. Clearly, Rabina's understanding of how text is constructed and what it is used for may differ radically from literacy practices in the classroom context. Once again the notion of a child-centred approach to learning as 'natural', and therefore value-free, is brought into question.

As seen in the drama episode, it is the interaction around the text as well as the text itself that confirms or challenges the children's developing understanding of what counts as literacy and what and who is valued. The teacher clearly has a difficult job in attempting to challenge a particular view of what is valued and desirable in 'princesses'. Some of the children seem reluctant to accept alternative views and comment that the story is 'stupid'. In spite of the teacher's attempts to 'disrupt' the stereotype, Rabina appears to recognize that she does not 'fit' the children's or the author's physical construction of a princess and slowly puts her hand down.

The notion of what counts and who has the power to maintain a reality is further demonstrated by the group working on the catering for Princess Smarty Pants' party. Although much of the food and drink suggested is likely to be within Rabina's experience – fish and chips, chicken sticks, hamburgers, sausages, cake, ice cream, lollies – there is no reference to the Asian food with which Rabina is most familiar. Is this construction of what is acceptable and desirable further reflected in Rabina's self-portrait, featuring pink skin colour and bright red cheeks?

Although collaborative small-group work is potentially a very powerful way of enabling children to share and explore differences, this is clearly not always the case. None of the children in Rabina's group appeared to be aware that as a Muslim, Rabina would not eat pork sausages and that the chicken would need to be prepared in a particular way. Thus, it can be seen that self-selection, free choice and group work can at worst marginalize, silence and compromise some children.

Conclusion

In this chapter I have tried to show that Rabina has developed a vast range of linguistic competences before coming to school. If this is true of Rabina, then it is likely that there will be many children like her. Rabina is developing an understanding of language and literacy through involvement in a range of social, cultural and religious contexts at home and in the wider community. The language and literacy practices that she experiences will influence her view of what 'counts' as literacy and how literacy is 'done'.

Second, I have argued that in order to enable Rabina to reach her potential these linguistic competences must be recognized and built on. Clearly this is not an easy task, especially if the teacher's view of what 'counts' as language and what is 'done' as literacy does not match, or is in conflict with, Rabina's understanding. In addition to this, the constraints of the National Curriculum may actually work against teachers' attempts to provide quality and equality in relation to children from ethnic minority groups, because of the marginalization of community languages.

Third, I have argued that the notion of a child-centred approach to learning does not necessarily lead to quality or equality. A child-centred approach, based on the idea that all children progress through universal stages of development, in which learning is seen as 'natural', runs the risk of:

• ignoring the influence of the context in which learning is taking place, which is value-laden and only easily accessible to those who share the same understandings and expectations;
• failing to recognize individual and cultural differences related to learning styles and patterns of interaction;
• denying the need to challenge language and behaviour that is seen as unacceptable and oppressive.

And yet there seem to be a number of dichotomies here. How can we encourage children to explore and experiment, to create their own understandings, while recognizing the need to make our expectations explicit for those children who may not share our assumptions about language and literacy? In addition to this, how can we build on children's knowledge and understanding, while challenging some of the concepts, particularly about race and gender, that children bring to school? Finally, how can we build on diversity within a system which appears, to some extent, to endorse and reward singular, predetermined views of the world?

In recognizing the complexity of teaching and learning, it is clear that there are no easy answers. The decisions we make depend upon our beliefs about learning, the children we teach and the context which brings us together. In conclusion, the following questions may help reflection on current quality and equality and raise issues for future practice.

Questions for discussion

The link between home and school

1 What does the school expect of children and parents before coming to school?
2 What underlying messages are implicit in the information that is given to parents either verbally or in the form of a booklet/ leaflet?
3 Is the relationship between home and school seen as a two-way process in which parents and teachers are equal partners?

Linguistic diversity in the classroom

4 What understandings and competences about language and literacy do you want the children you work with to develop?
5 Does this include the recognition, sharing and extension of the linguistic resources children bring to school?
6 How can you incorporate and extend the children's linguistic repertoire through the development of language and literacy?
7 How can you involve all the children in your class in learning about linguistic diversity?

Patterns of interaction in the classroom

8 What values and assumptions are implicit in the way you organize learning, the curriculum content and the resources you use?

9 Do you recognize and respond to the linguistic, cultural and religious conventions of the children you are working with?

10 Does your planning and practice include ways of helping children to reflect on the way in which language shapes identity and defines reality?

11 How do you deal with conflicts of interests within the classroom and school when value systems seem to be in opposition to each other?

Suggested further reading

Baker, C. (1993) *Foundations of Bilingual Education and Bilingualism*. London: Taylor & Francis.

Edwards, C., Moorhouse, J. and Widlake, S. (1988) 'Language or English? The Needs of Bilingual Pupils', in Jones, M. and West, A. (eds), *Learning Me Your Language: Perspectives on the Teaching of English*. London: Mary Glasgow.

Raychaudhuri, S. (1989) 'Children off the Edge – Language in the National Curriculum and the Bilingual Child', in *Language Matters*, No. 3. London: Centre for Learning in Primary Education.

Skutnabb-Kangas, T. and Cummins J. (1988) *Minority Education from Shame to Struggle*. Clevedon, PA: Multilingual Matters.

7

People matter: The role of adults in providing a quality learning environment for the early years

Chris Marsh

> all adults working with under fives need to . . . build relationships of trust with children so that they develop the confidence to take risks in a secure setting and can accept, use and overcome minor failures . . .
>
> (DES 1990: 12)

As this quotation illustrates, successful relationships provide the basis for quality teaching and learning. A publication from the National Primary Centre (1989: 1) sums it up thus: 'If you get the relationships right, you are well on the way to creating an effective learning environment'. Relationships between educators and children are therefore recognized as being crucial to children's emotional security and ability to benefit from the educational environment, children's ability and confidence in developing relationships with their peers, and educators' sense of professional achievement.

In addition to forming positive relationships with children, early years educators also have to forge effective links with the children's parents and with professional colleagues. As Hurst (1987) points out, 'adapting to school is a major experience for child and parent . . . [and] on the success of this endeavour rests the success of the child's future experiences of education'. It is not surprising therefore that the National Association of Inspectors and Educational Advisers (NAIEA 1985: 11) stated that 'high quality nursery education depends primarily upon the quality of the staff employed'. This raises the question of what characteristics a person needs to be a successful educator. The *Review of Initial Teacher Training in Northern Ireland* (DENI 1993: 5) defines the following professional competences as characterizing the successful teacher: professional knowledge, professional development, personal development, communication and relationships, synthesis and application. To be viewed as 'successful', communication and relationships necessitate:

> A person who is able to communicate easily and effectively; able to establish and maintain constructive relationships with children, colleagues, parents and others; [and is] sensitive to the emotional dimension of interaction with children and others.

The quality of relationships within the classroom and outside in the wider educational context is thus a central prerequisite to successful teaching (Dowling 1992; Pollard and Tann 1987).

The role of the early years teacher, and that of the nursery teacher in particular, is rendered more complex by the fact that he/she works with one or more professional nursery nurses. In the case of a nursery teacher this usually means sharing the teaching area and duties with one or more other professionals for the majority of one's working time. Apart from the demands this raises in terms of team work, communication and relationships, there may be a sense of discontent on the part of nursery nurses in that, although they are qualified professionals working alongside teachers, there are major differences in financial reward and salary structure, and there is almost no possibility for career enhancement within the educational system. It is a part of the nursery teacher's job to ensure that these grievances on the part of their nursery nurse colleagues do not undermine the successful working relationships and life of the nursery or school (Heaslip 1987; Yeomans 1989).

Relationships are clearly crucial to successful education yet relatively little has been written on this aspect. The quality of classroom relationships is:

considered to be important in facilitating learning, in providing both teacher and children with a sense of self-fulfilment
and, in addition ... often seen as the basis for a positive,
purposefully disciplined working atmosphere. Yet, classroom
relationships is a subject which seems to defy analysis. Perhaps this is because relationships are the product of such very
particular, complex and subtle personal interactions between
teachers and children.

(Pollard and Tann 1987: 61)

While this is undoubtedly true, it is necessary to try to ascertain
more tangible factors which contribute to quality in order to clarify
how we can strive to attain it in our classrooms. Tizard (1986) suggested three main criteria conducive to quality child care: familiarity, responsiveness and attachment. Familiarity was seen as
dependent upon the regular involvement of the same children with
the same adults. Responsiveness relates to the intuitive response
of the adult who treats all children as individuals and interacts
with them on that premise. However, the intuitiveness is that of
the trained professional as opposed to a mere sense of guesswork.
Attachment results from the establishing of a reciprocal emotional
bond between the adult and the child. Such attachment can also
develop between one child and another. As Watt (1987: 11) concludes in relation to Tizard's findings:

Good care, she would seem to be arguing, is the prerequisite
of good education since it is only from this sound secure
framework of social relationships that young children can gain
confidence in themselves and build up positive attitudes to
their own learning.

Rogers (1969) posits three similar qualities necessary for warm,
'person-centred' relationships to be established: acceptance, genuineness, and empathy. This requires the educator to possess a
genuine acceptance of children as they are, and to be able to view
situations from their perspective. Rogers's qualities for purposeful
adult–child relationships could apply equally to the relationships
of educators working collaboratively. For successful and harmoni-
ous team work to take place all professionals need to have a consensus of values and a commitment to the children in their care
and to their families.

In order to define the role of adults in providing a quality learning environment more systematically, it is useful to explore some of the theoretical observations noted above in the context of a particular early years setting, while recognizing that the observations have general applicability to other educational contexts and age ranges. Similarly, it is important to try to break down the issue of 'relationships' into various dimensions of working practice. This, in turn, can lead to a synthesis of theoretical analysis and observation in order to produce some statements of good practice (expressed via a self-critical framework) against which the operation of different educational settings may be analysed and compared.

The following analysis seeks to achieve this objective via a case study of an individual nursery, observed in the light of current theoretical writings on relationships and analysed in terms of distinct dimensions of working practice. It then leads on to the production of a 'quality framework' for assessing relationships within educational establishments.

The case study centred on a nursery school in a LEA in North West England and involved two researchers working as both participant and non-participant observers and interviewing the parents of the children attending the school in order to gain their views of the nursery and the service it was providing.

The nursery school is located in an urban area close to the town centre. Many of the residents in the area have been born and grown up in the area and their children and grandchildren have attended the nursery. While by no means all the parents have lived in this area for many years, a significant proportion have relatives who have lived within a small radius of the town centre.

The adult role in practice

Observations in the case-study nursery, of adults working with the children, and interviews with parents and discussions with staff, showed that the qualities suggested as contributing towards effective relationships postulated by both Tizard (1986) and Rogers (1969) could be analysed in terms of four distinct yet interrelated categories of practice:

- relationships between educators and parents, including written communication between school and home;

- educator–child relationships;
- team work and ethos; and
- management, leadership and organization.

Relationships between educators and parents

Parents' first impressions are likely to be based on the physical environment and the work and notices on display, as these will be encountered early in a visit. The messages which are given from displays of children's work and the wording of notices providing information set the general tone of the establishment and should aim to establish a friendly and welcoming atmosphere. Letters from school to parents are also important in terms of the tone they set as well as the information which they aim to impart. All too often negative messages are given. As Jowett *et al.* (1991: 136) comment:

> So many of the school handbooks and other documentation for parents gathered during this research were not particularly informative and were written in a style that could by itself easily discourage parents from making contact: booklets that started with a list of school rules rather than a welcoming note were obvious examples.

They concluded:

> The intention has to be to produce material which is pitched at the right level, so that parents feel neither patronised nor overwhelmed and demoralised – and that is a difficult balance to strike.

The latter point is one with which the nursery headteacher and I can sympathize, having struggled with the wording of a letter explaining the purpose and intention of the interviews to be held with parents.

Some schools and LEAs have home school teachers, or teachers from nursery or reception classes who undertake a home visit prior to a child beginning at the nursery or in the reception class. In this way relationships can begin to be established in surroundings familiar to the child, and parents can discuss any concerns or raise any queries they may have. Where a visiting system does operate it can be arranged so that the educator who will have most contact with the child in school is the one who undertakes the visit. This link with one adult can then be fostered by that person being readily available on any visits prior to the child starting on a regular basis. At the case-study nursery each child in a specific family group has a visit to the nursery with a parent or carer, where they are welcomed by their family group leader who will teach those children for parts of each day in a smaller group situation for story-time and snack-time. These children then start attending on the same day. This gives the children and their carers opportunities to know other children and parents belonging to their family group. If a child has siblings who have previously attended the nursery the younger child will join the family group to which his/her older siblings belonged, giving the educator and parents the possibility of developing a longer-term relationship. A parent toddler group held on the nursery premises is also beneficial in familiarizing children with the building and the educators prior to their starting nursery officially.

The parents who were interviewed were highly in favour of the family group system. They found it beneficial to have a particularly strong bond with one educator although if that person were not available they were quite prepared to discuss issues with other adults. The friendliness of the educators and their enthusiasm for working with children was frequently commented upon. As one mother put it: 'They're very friendly and approachable but not to the point where you lose respect for them.' This ability to distance oneself professionally when necessary was observed on occasions where a parent had not kept the nursery staff informed regarding a child's health or the school to which the child would be transferring for the next school year.

The educator who ran the parent toddler group was also involved in the nursery. Her work in both situations gave her opportunities to see the progress and development of her previous toddler group children and provided a familiar friendly face for those children new to nursery who had previously attended the toddler group. It was also evident that she, in common with other staff, shared the school ethos and philosophy regarding the care of children and accepted standards of behaviour.

Another factor which the parents regarded as important was that until recently when two staff moved (one due to her partner's

job change necessitating a move to another area, another for promotion), the staff had all been at the school for several years. The
headteacher in particular had worked there for many years and
this was frequently commented upon in positive terms by parents
who regarded her as the stabilizing influence of the establishment.
Several parents commented upon the nursery teacher leaving; they
felt it was a fault in the education system that a teacher had to
move on to further her promotion prospects when that teacher
was happy where she was and had successfully established a rapport
with children, parents and colleagues. Low staff turnover was clearly
regarded as desirable by the parents. This was especially significant as the headteacher was keenly aware of the need for each
member of staff to complement the team not just in curriculum
areas but also in contributing to the ethos of the school and in
forming positive relationships with peers. This supportiveness of
staff members towards each other and their agreement regarding
the importance of fostering positive relationships with parents
provides a welcoming atmosphere which is noted and appreciated
by parents and other visitors alike. As Richman and McGuire
(1988) state:

> where staff are confident and encouraging to parents, there
> are measurable benefits to the children. In other words, the
> overall style of nursery organization is clearly related to staff
> behaviour [and depends upon a common ethos and shared
> agreement among staff] and this, together with staff–child
> ratios, affects the level and quality of adult–child interaction.

Janice Adams, in Chapter 5, and Helen Strahan, in Chapter 8,
both reinforce this important point.

Educator–child relationships

The success of educator–child relationships is certainly enhanced
by positive relationships and open communication between educators and parents. An example of positive relationships where
the needs of both the parent and the child were catered for was
observed in the case-study nursery. A mother arrived to collect
her daughter looking very upset and flustered. The headteacher
took the parent to another room to discuss the problem privately

while the staff engaged the interest of the child, playing with her and involving her so that she was content to stay with them rather than go with her mother. Staff, individually and collectively, need to be sensitive in all their interactions with pupils, parents and colleagues. Dowling (1992) makes the point that while personal qualities such as humour, empathy and a genuine interest and concern for people help form the basis for successful relationships, these qualities are far from easy to teach and often only become apparent when an individual educator fails to possess them. This has important implications for the interview and selection procedures for teaching and nursery nursing. These personal qualities are often highly valued by headteachers, too, who look for evidence of the individual's ability to build successful relationships when interviewing for staff vacancies.

Sensitive interaction between an adult and a child in the case-study nursery was often demonstrated by the adult sensing the child's need or potential unease and responding before the child became upset. For instance, one child looked slightly distressed and unwilling to become involved in any of the activities as her mother prepared to leave. An adult took the child by the hand and together they went and sat at an activity. The adult placed the girl on her lap, put her arms round her and chatted informally while engaging her in the activity alongside several other children. Within three minutes the child was settled and engrossed in the activity. Shortly after this the adult lifted the girl off her lap and went to join another group. The girl continued her play at the table with her peers. Such sensitive interactions minimize the instances of children becoming distraught; in addition, by adopting a caring role more akin to that of a parent it is possible that the adult's language will be more detailed than the brief, often perfunctory, exchanges fairly typical of educational settings (Tizard and Hughes 1984). Where adults know their children well and know which ones are most likely to react adversely or to be insecure or frightened in particular circumstances, they can give the children their support, often pre-empting or at least minimizing their fear or discomfort. Thus where educators succeed in establishing very positive caring relationships with children the number of disruptions to purposeful teaching and learning are significantly reduced (Pollard and Tann 1987). In Chapter 9, Brenda Griffin reinforces this point in describing the role of the 'key worker' in the 'educare' of the under-threes.

Care for one another is demonstrated in the case-study nursery indirectly by the educators providing positive role models in their interactions with pupils, parents and colleagues, and directly by the adults' discussion with children about how they are interacting with each other. Positive praise is frequently given in both small- and large-group situations where children have worked co-operatively and tried to help each other. Equally, where children are not being considerate with each other this is discussed with them, with the adults providing suggestions of ways in which they can help each other and why this makes everyone feel happier.

In the case-study nursery, the time and care devoted to fostering positive relationships between the children showed in terms of their positive interactions with each other, both within particular friendships, and on a more general basis. Examples of the latter included an instance where James was struggling with a jigsaw. Ricky went and sat beside him and helped. James smiled a 'thank you' after they had completed it together. No verbal interaction occurred but they both looked pleased with themselves on completing the task. The parents and the researchers both commented on the frequency of children helping each other in this way, especially later in the school year when relationships had had time to consolidate. For example, on seeing a child hovering, anxious to do some drawing at an already full table, Ashley said: 'When I've coloured in my castle you can have my place.' On another occasion, Jennifer was using coloured wooden shapes to make a picture. Through discussion with an adult Jennifer decided she did not have enough blue squares to make the long body section she wanted to. Gareth approached the adult: 'Here's a blue one.' Unfortunately it was a blue triangle not a square, but he *was* trying to help! On yet another occasion, Wesley and Gareth were playing with identical models made from construction materials. An adult asked who had made his model first. Wesley announced that he had. The adult continued: 'Then Gareth did one the same?' Wesley replied, 'No, I made it for him', then they moved on, continuing their imaginative play based on the aeroplanes Wesley had made.

In the case-study nursery the adults' concern that everyone

treated each other with consideration, respect and courtesy, was mirrored in the children's interactions with one another and with adults. The children were very kind and thoughtful towards each other (most of the time) and staff praised this behaviour. Where there were any disagreements between children staff sorted them out immediately with the individuals concerned. One person who was interviewed mentioned her child being scared of another child. She had mentioned this to a member of staff: 'There's never been any problem since.' An underlying theme throughout the school year is 'being nice to one another, sharing and taking turns'. Children's behaviour towards each other assumes a high priority whatever the activities on offer, and sometimes activities are chosen to encourage cooperation. The relationships between adults and children and between the children themselves are generally very positive and this is reflected in a calm, happy and productive working atmosphere.

Team work and ethos

Positive and effective relationships within the classroom will permeate outside into the wider school environment; equally, purposeful and positive relationships within the school generally can help establish similar relationships within each classroom as a certain expectation of behaviour is already implicit. This supportive school ethos is particularly valuable to newcomers to the establishment, whether they are teachers, nursery nurses, pupils or parents. A shared ethos and a team work approach also help provide security and continuity during times of change such as staff changes and the beginning of a school year. For fruitful team work to take place, as well as a sharing of values, aims and ideals, staff need to have highly developed interpersonal skills to enable them to develop and sustain positive relationships with their colleagues. Such skills do not develop in isolation or automatically, and yet, ironically, many teachers do not receive any training in the acquisition of such skills until they consider courses in management for promotion possibilities. There are clear implications here for the training of all professionals working with young children

Team work in an early years setting, in nurseries especially, usually means teachers and nursery nurses planning and implementing the curriculum together. Thus nursery teachers and managers need to be adept at leading and managing a team, skills which are not always developed during the professional's initial training. The training of nursery teachers and nursery nurses varies in type and duration, the qualifications necessary for entry, and the minimum age for beginning training. Heaslip (1987: 34) states: 'If the two professions are to be complementary, greater knowledge of each others training can only lead to clearer understanding of each other's roles, skills and strengths.' Clift *et al.* (1980) emphasized that in their research the nursery teachers usually perceived themselves in the role of team leader and acted accordingly. The continued development of multiprofessional training is a clearly identified need, together with the need to safeguard the graduate status of the early years teacher as leader of a professional team.

Yeomans (1989) discusses the difficulties inherent in the relationship between teachers and nursery nurses, which he refers to as 'a partnership of unequals' where people work in close face-to-face relationships with each other. Yeomans points out that because of these close relationships early years teachers require additional and more highly developed interpersonal skills than their later years colleagues. In the case-study nursery Yeomans's (1989: 28) comment certainly applied: 'The cohesive effect of belonging to a group of people who find that they can and do depend and rely on one another means that issues such as pay and status seldom surface.' As the staff were aware, however, this depends upon successful team work where roles, on a day-to-day basis, are not too clearly delineated and everyone is prepared to help as and where necessary in the event of something unforeseen occurring. This also necessitates effective and up-to-date communication among staff in terms of children's needs, behaviour and learning experiences, as well as on the curriculum to be covered. Keeping all staff informed on these issues is essential for the smooth running of the establishment and the personal and professional satisfaction of the individuals. As Laishley (1983: 166) comments, 'irrespective of role and status adults need to experience the positive support of colleagues and have the opportunity to talk with colleagues so that they can work consistently with children [aiming] towards similar goals'.

The case-study nursery had recently experienced staff changes and two new staff were to replace the previous temporary appointments in the new school year. The headteacher was enthusiastic about the possibilities for whole-school staff discussion on issues of curriculum, management and organization, and before the children started school, time had been set aside for the staff to get to know each other and plan collaboratively the topics they would teach and how they would organize and manage the teaching environment. In this way new staff were able to share decisions with the existing staff relating to possible reorganization of materials and the organization of the working day. Developing and nurturing the new staff team was an important issue to the headteacher, and through discussions about the teaching and learning which would take place the ethos and aims of the nursery would be clarified and shared by all the staff, helping to consolidate their group identity and sense of belonging.

Nias *et al.* (1989) suggest that more needs to be done in in-service education to help teachers perceive and understand the notion of organizational culture and its impact on schools. This is especially important for staff new to a school and can be influential in their successful acculturation into an establishment. The case-study nursery demonstrated a high degree of awareness of the importance of the selection of staff, considering personal qualities, interaction and leadership skills, as well as curriculum expertise, and of the significance of the first few weeks in a new establishment for the newly arrived professionals and their colleagues. Consequently, the staff had met socially before the new staff took up their appointments, and staff development time had been set aside before the children started back at school so that the staff could begin to establish relationships with each other and discuss professional issues which would be affecting them all in both the short and longer term. Some of these issues, such as curriculum expertise, were already associated with particular individuals, but many issues concerning organization of the classrooms and the school day were to be discussed and thought through as a whole staff so that newcomers' opinions and ideas would be accepted and acted upon immediately. In this way, both individually and collectively, the staff would assume responsibility for the curriculum, the environment and the successful running of the nursery on a day-to-day basis. The success or otherwise of these decisions would be the subject of future team meetings, with discussions concerning how to improve current practice. And the achievements of the staff would be viewed as both individual and collective professional growth.

Management, leadership and organization

The headteacher in a nursery school and, to a lesser extent, the teacher in charge of a nursery class, have a responsibility for establishing the ethos of the educational setting, and making sure that the educational objectives and goals of positive communication are successfully achieved so that children, staff and parents work together to contribute to a valuable and meaningful experience for all those involved. Nias *et al.* (1989) concluded that headteachers and other leaders in schools are very significant figures; they have to undertake the complex and dynamic task of leadership, in addition to the more tangible elements of their job. In addition to leading and maintaining the culture of the school, the head's role is crucial in establishing and fostering positive relationships among staff. Heads, through their informal behaviour towards staff, in negotiation and liaison regarding issues, help to set a pattern for relationships based on mutual respect. In addition, Nias noted, heads did not hesitate to use their formal authority if they felt this would be beneficial. The heads in this study did not hesitate to use their formal authority if they felt this would be beneficial.

Both the ability to adopt a position of authority and the positive style of interaction and negotiation were evident in the head's role in the case-study nursery. Her proactive stance and willingness to negotiate and liaise with staff and parents, and her ability to provide a positive role model and inspire and enthuse others, were frequently observed by the researchers, as well as being commented upon by parents in their interviews. The head also welcomed students into the team and succeeded in making everyone involved feel a valued and respected team member with worthwhile contributions to make. This positive leadership affected the organization of the nursery and its running and created an eagerness to work together and to put forward suggestions, knowing that contributions would be valued, considered, and acted upon if the rest of the team were in agreement. For example, students working in the school had considerable freedom to plan, develop, teach and introduce activities with the children. After their teaching they assessed the children's learning with staff and learnt from this experience how to plan activities and structure them in order to ensure the greatest benefit to the children. Thus through success-ful management and positive leadership the nursery was organ-ized in such a way that every adult was purposefully involved and fully participating.

Summary

In relation to the case-study nursery the criteria of familiarity, res-ponsiveness and attachment (Tizard 1986) are clearly exhibited, helping to provide an atmosphere and environment which is con-ducive to both quality care and quality education. While the family group system provides opportunities for children to develop a more intense relationship with one adult, the children also have opportunities for interaction with all the other educators during parts of the day so that if their family group educator is absent they will be familiar with other adults. Examples of the adults' responsiveness have been given in the case study: attachment to adults was clearly demonstrated by numerous observations of instances where children leaned on or snuggled up to adults, shared smiles or jokes, or rushed to meet them on entering the nursery. Similar attachments occurred between children – for example, while listening to a story on the carpet, Thomas put his arm around Luke with all the ease of child at home rather than at school.

Similarly, the qualities of acceptance, genuineness and empathy (Rogers 1969) were demonstrated between adults and children and between adults. One could argue that acceptance is a neces-sary prerequisite for successful familiarity and ease on the adult's part, while genuineness facilitates responsiveness and empathy facilitates attachment. Through diligent selection of staff who possess these qualities, together with well-planned team-building activities and a shared ethos, the case-study nursery succeeded in developing, fostering and enhancing successful relationships between educators, pupils and parents.

Promoting good practice

A recent report by OFSTED (1993c) emphasized that the curricu-lum includes not only the National Curriculum and other subjects but also factors which contribute to the school ethos, such as the quality of relationships and the organization and management of classes. Similarly the *Junior School Report* (ILEA 1986) identified several factors which contribute to the quality of an establishment. Among these were an effective headteacher of high calibre, a supportive deputy head, and a good staff climate. Thus relationships within any establishment not only contribute to its success but also help to make it, in terms of effectiveness, more than the mere sum of its parts.

In order to assess the effectiveness and quality of relationships in an establishment or in an individual classroom, some sort of framework is necessary so that we can pinpoint current areas of strength and weakness. It is then possible, through observation and discussion, to define those elements which contribute to the strengths and successes, and to try to identify ways in which to enhance those areas where we feel least successful. The following quality framework (based on the empirical observation and academic research described above) is an attempt to provide an initial structure for practitioners to consider, adapt and alter to fit their own needs for their particular setting.

A quality framework for assessing relationships within an establishment

The following sources were used in compiling this quality framework: Balageur *et al.* (1992); Northern Group of Advisers (1992); Sheffield LEA (1992); McCail (1991); Braun (1992); and Curtis and Hevey (1992).

1 Relationships with children
   (a) General
      How is acceptable behaviour reinforced and rewarded?
      How is inappropriate behaviour dealt with?
      Is this consistent between educators?
      How are children encouraged to develop a positive self-image?
      Do children have opportunities to work:
         alone?
         in pairs?
         in groups?

Are co-operative activities encouraged and planned for?
What measures are taken to make meal-time an enjoyable social occasion?
How are children's individual needs and abilities catered for?
Do all the adults participate effectively in the children's activities?

(b) *Interactions*
Is there evidence that the adult, when interacting with a child:
Gives the child time to listen and respond?
Values children's contributions and provides positive comments and praise?
Does not attempt to force a response if the child is not yet secure enough (for example, is new to the setting, or has English as a second or third language)?
Provides a friendly commentary on the activity?
Asks open-ended questions?
Listens responsively and attentively?
Provides supportive body language and gestures?
Possesses a high degree of awareness of what is going on and regularly reviews the extent to which children are involved in their tasks?
Keeps children informed of events and changes which are going to take place?

(c) *Children's relationships with adults*
Do children approach adults confidently?
Do children seek adult participation?
Do children perceive adults as partners in play?
Do children demonstrate a degree of independence?

(d) *Children's relationships with their peers*
In children's relationships with their peers, is there evidence that:
They usually treat each other with respect?
They are supportive of each other and each other's contributions in work and play?
They share and take turns reasonably often, allowing for their emotional and developmental levels?
They respond positively to most other children and adults most of the time?

They exhibit enthusiasm and positive attitudes most of the time?

They have some degree of choice over their playmates and the activities which they undertake?

They enjoy coming to school and being there?

2 Relationships with other educators

(a) General

Do individuals find it difficult working with adults compared to working with children?

If there are difficulties, how can these be lessened or overcome?

Do all educators have opportunities to proffer suggestions and ideas?

Are decisions joint and democratic?

Is time made for whole-staff training and meetings to share ideas and disseminate information?

Is a whole-school approach seen as important and as an aim to strive for?

Do staff have clearly defined areas of responsibility for curriculum and materials so that new staff and parent helpers know whom to approach for help?

Is the expertise of each member of staff valued?

How is this shown?

Are there opportunities for all staff to experience professional development within the establishment?

Are these opportunities realized?

Are there opportunities for staff to attend courses and visit other establishments?

Are individuals asked to disseminate information after attending courses and visiting other establishments?

How are staff kept informed about daily events, meetings, child health problems, and so on?

(b) Interactions

In the adult's relationships with other educators, is there evidence that the adult:

Treats others with respect?

Explains why situations (unforeseen or at short notice) are occurring?

Values other contributions and comments and either acts upon them or explains why it is not feasible to do so?

Gives praise where appropriate?
Makes critical comments privately, explaining the reasons for the inappropriateness of actions?
Operates a collaborative approach with adults supporting each other in carrying out their respective roles?
Is there a common ethos implicit to observers?

3 Relationships with parents

(a) General

How are children and parents inducted?
How are parents informed about the events and activities you plan?
Are parental feedback and views on the work done by their children encouraged?
If so, how?
How is the atmosphere and environment in the school made welcoming?
How easy is it for parents to find their way about the school and to know whom to contact?
What has been done to facilitate this?
Is written information available in the home languages of all the pupils?
Is there a whole-school approach to discipline and the development of effective relationships?
Is this written down as a policy document, or in a booklet about the school?
If so, who has been involved in deciding upon this policy?
Are parents informed about it, and how?
Where can parents discuss concerns with staff?
Is privacy ensured?
Are staff available before or after sessions and at the beginning and end of the school day?
Is there a parents' room or an area where parents can meet for a chat?
If so, is it well used? By whom and for what purposes?
Could its use be developed further?
If so, how?
How often are parents' evenings?
Are these timed to fit in with parents' needs?
Does the timing during the school year fit in with parents' needs to find out about their children's progress?

Could such occasions be made more hospitable, for example, by providing parents as well as staff with tea or coffee? Are opportunities available between parents' evenings to discuss a child's progress? Have you canvassed parents' opinions on any or all of these issues within the last two years?

(b) Interactions

In the educator's relationships with parents is there evidence that the educator:

Treats them with respect?

Gives time to parents' concerns and treats them confidentially?

Acts sensitively towards their needs (for example, tries to provide information or contact numbers, takes the parent somewhere private to talk when appropriate) and values their comments and contributions?

Acts upon parents' suggestions/comments if these are appropriate, and, where they are not, explains why?

Is non-judgemental as far as this is professionally possible?

Appreciates parents' concerns while regarding the child as the first priority professionally?

(c) Parental involvement

Is parental expertise used?

How is it encouraged and organized?

Do parents take prime responsibility in organizing any activities?

What is the role of staff in these activities?

Do parents help in organizing any activities?

Do parents help with children in the classroom or around the school?

Is guidance given prior to working with children?

Is feedback sought afterwards? What form does this take?

Are parents involved in school visits?

Is guidance given prior to the outing?

Are parents involved in record-keeping?

Do they have opportunities to add their comments?

Is parental involvement in school monitored and evaluated?

If so, how, by whom, and for what purposes?

Are there opportunities for parents to suggest ways of increasing their involvement in school? Have you any future aims or plans regarding parental involvement in your establishment?

Suggested further reading

Braun, D. (1992) 'Working with Parents' in Pugh, G., *Contemporary Issues in the Early Years*. London: Paul Chapman.

Hurst, V. (1987) 'Parents and Professionals: Partnership in Early Childhood Education' in Blenkin G.M. and Kelly A.V. (eds), *Early Childhood Education*. London: Paul Chapman.

National Primary Centre (1989) *Relationships*. Practical Issues in Primary Education No. 3. Oxford: National Primary Centre.

Nias, J., Southworth, G. and Yeomans, R. (1989) *Staff Relationships in the Primary School*. London: Cassell.

OFSTED (1993) *Well Managed Classes in Primary Schools*. A Report from the Office of HM's Chief Inspector of Schools. London: HMSO.

Pollard, A. and Tann, S. (1987) *Reflective Teaching in the Primary School*. London: Paul Chapman.

8

'You feel like you belong': Establishing partnerships between parents and educators

Helen Strahan

> What is always necessary ... is the establishment of a part-
> nership between parents and other educators. For this to be
> effective, there must be mutual understanding and respect, a
> continuing dialogue and sharing of expertise and information.
>
> (DES 1990: 13)

There are many obvious outward signs that Queens Road Primary
School regards itself as an important part of the community and
welcomes parental involvement in the school. The building is
used by various community groups outside school hours. There is
a 'Joint Community Forum' in which the school is involved and
where ideas are shared. Community family nights are held at the
school. Access is clearly marked and the entrance hall is welcoming and full of well-presented information about Queens Road, its
aims and activities. Photographs of children and staff engaged in
activities both in and outside school and examples of children's
work are displayed. The school brochure is illustrated by the children. The first page says what sort of school Queens Road aims to
be.

- A secure, stimulating and challenging environment within
  which both children and staff can grow, learn and achieve
  success in an atmosphere of mutual respect.
- A school with high expectations of both children and staff,
  which enjoys striving for quality in all aspects of school life.

- A school that works in partnership with staff, parents and the community for the good of all our children.
  At the heart of this statement are people. We believe that our school is concerned with the development of people to their full potential.

A person-centred approach is manifested in the rest of the brochure. The emphasis is on admissions, ethos and curriculum and how all parties can work together; lists and official business are kept to a minimum. The last section of text is entitled 'Home and School Working in Partnership' and concludes: 'We look forward to a fruitful relationship between school and home, with us working together for the benefit of all the children.'

It is how these aims are achieved in practice, together with the opportunities for and constraints on partnership, that are explored in this chapter. It is not about short-cuts to good practice, rather it is an exploration from an interactionist perspective of how a particular group of people have constructed and negotiated home–school relationships. It is an attempt to look at the complexity of the search for quality in this particular aspect of school life.

Queens Road's local area consists of an old village centre surrounded by four large council estates built between the 1950s and early 1980s to house the former residents of crumbling inner-city blocks of flats. The school is part of the newest estate and was actually completed eleven years ago – before many of the houses were finished. It has grown with the estate, establishing its role within the community just as the families it serves have done.

As an outsider in the school I was able to observe the actual dealings of parents, children and staff, and to talk with them about the meanings they attached to these interactions and their feelings about them. In order to present some of the data to the reader interestingly and accessibly I have 'fictionalized' it. The places, the people and the things they say, although anonymized, are real; it is only the way in which a series of events and interactions have been combined into a chronological narrative that is fiction.

Winter (1991: 252) provides an explanation of what fiction means in this context:

> In response to a mass of data, the researcher makes a set of general notes elucidating an initial set of themes. S/he then composes a story which attempts to provide a summary of the relationships between (and the implications of) these themes.

So this chapter does not pretend to be a detailed research report in the usual sense, nevertheless the story presents some of the actual lived experience of the participants. The discussion that follows it explores some underlying themes and principles. The chapter concludes with some further questions which could possibly be used in conjunction with the story for staff development purposes.

The story

It is an ordinary Thursday morning at Queens Road Primary School. The day has started quietly; all are going about their normal business. Only two children have had to come in through the front door because they were late.

At 10.30 the headteacher's office door is roughly pushed open. Tom Fraser looks up from the pile of papers he has been trying to deal with since Monday and sees Joe Shaw standing on the threshold. Before he can say anything, Mr Shaw launches into a long, angry diatribe. Tom listens and then finally interrupts:

'I understand that you're upset, Mr Shaw, but I'm not quite clear about all the facts. Why don't you sit down and then we can talk about how I can help you.'

During the course of the subsequent conversation it transpires that this parent is worried by two things. What he is angry about is what he sees as a serious shortcoming in the school's discipline policy:

'I've told them all if anyone hits you, you hit them back – and then our Wayne gets punished for it.'

Tom's response to this is to agree that this policy seems logical and quite appropriate for the street when there are no adults around. He then goes on to state that this approach will never be allowed in school; that one of the principles on which the school discipline policy is based is that all children and adults should be spoken to and treated with respect, and that this rules out physical violence of *any* sort. The children all know that if anyone hits them they must tell an adult, not hit back. The class teacher was quite right to make Wayne spend the last five minutes of breaktime with her. Joe listens attentively to this exposition, but says he is still not sure about it. Tom suggests that he reserves judgement until Wayne, who is still in reception, has been in school a bit longer.

They then move on to talk about Joe's other concern. He already has an older child who is attending special school and he is worried that Wayne may have similar problems. He wants him to join the 'special reading class'. Tom explains that the special needs support teachers work with children who are having particular difficulties and that, so far, Wayne appears to be progressing quite normally for a five-year-old. He asks Joe if he enjoys reading with Wayne at home. Joe says that he does, but that he often does not have time and that he thinks the books are too easy with too many pictures. Tom suggests that he makes an arrangement to come in and talk to Wayne's class teacher about his reading. She will be able to spend time explaining the school's approach and also talk to him about how she is monitoring Wayne's progress.

Although Tom is aware that it is 11 o'clock and that by now Mrs Carter, a 'new' parent, is probably waiting to see him, he asks Joe a general question about how things are going. (He knows that the family is having all sorts of financial problems and he has been asked for advice in the past.) Joe reveals that, although the money matters were gradually being sorted out, things have become very difficult in the last two weeks because his wife has left him with the kids. The two men discuss the implications of this situation at some length.

While they have been talking, Sharon Carter has entered by the clearly marked front door. (She is relieved to be able to find her way in so easily – when she first visited her son's present school she spent ages trying to find the correct entrance and ended up nervously asking if she could come through the kitchen.) She goes to the nearby secretary's office and explains that she has an appointment to see the headteacher. Anne Jackson, the secretary, smiles at her and says:

'Oh yes, we're expecting you. Mr Fraser may be a few minutes, he's got somebody with him, but please take a seat in the hall. Would you like a cup of tea or coffee?'

Mrs Carter sits down on a comfortable seat in the pleasantly furnished entrance hall. She looks around and her eyes are drawn to the large frames on the walls which appear to be full of interesting photographs and writing. Anne brings her a cup of coffee and asks about her children and where she is going to be living. Very soon the phone summons Anne back to the office, and Sharon notices something called the 'Queens Road Report 1992/3' on the low table in front of her; she is quickly engrossed in reading it. In fact it takes her some time to realize that this newspaper, with its short snappy articles illustrated with children's drawings and photos, is actually the governors' annual report.

While Sharon is reading several children, both infants and juniors, pass through. All say hello, and two stop and engage in conversation about the photo on the front page of the report. Three adults appear; they are talking about the best way of helping a group of children given what they have observed in class this morning. One goes into the staffroom and the other two sit down near Sharon with their cups of coffee. They say hello and ask:

'Are you waiting to see the Head?'

'Yes' says Sharon. 'We're moving here next week and I wanted to come and see the school. My mum lives just down the road.'

After some conversation about the number and ages of her children and the exact location of the new house and the identity of her mum, her two companions move on to tell Sharon about the school and what they do there.

'I've been involved in the school for about four years' says Jane. 'I first started coming in helping reading and that, then I did the toy library for reception. Then they asked me to do the library. Jackie's not been coming that long though.'

'No. My daughter's only in the nursery. I help in the juniors, I like hearing them read and I do the toy library in the nursery. It was Mrs Jones who first asked me and I thought, well, I've got lots of free time at home; if it helps them I don't mind doing it. I love coming here now, I know more about how the school works and I see more than the nursery in action. I know where Kelly will be in the future.'

'Yes, and it's a friendly school and they're casual, they're not looking at you every minute and you feel like you belong.'

'The staff are nice, they've always been all right with me – if they're all right with you, then you're all right with them.'

'Come and have a look at these pictures. Whenever anything's happened they make a nice display and put up the photos and everything. This is when they went to Wales and the writing always says something about the work and the aims of the school ... That's my daughter there, she wrote a story ten pages long and she was thrilled to bits and the teacher was too.'

Just then they are interrupted by a voice saying 'Hiya, mum'. It is Jane's daughter, Emma. Jane greets her and says:

'We were just talking about you and that story you wrote. This is Sharon. Her little boy and girl are coming here soon.'
'Will you come and help like my mum does?' asks Emma.
'Maybe, but I'm not sure I'd know what to do.'
'You can read with the children and help with the work and mum helps us with the library. You pick a book and she takes the ticket out and puts it in a box. I like to bring her a cup of tea but sometimes other children go, so I can't do it all the time.'
Just then the head and Joe Shaw come round the corner from the office.
'Thanks for coming, Mr Shaw.'
'Bye now. Thanks for your help.'
Turning back from the front door, Tom Fraser smiles at the three women and Emma who gives him a note from her teacher. Tom chuckles as he reads this, winks at Emma and says: 'Tell Mrs Andrews "Yes, just this once!"' Emma laughs and heads back to her class. Tom greets the two parents he knows by name and then shakes hands with Sharon.
'Hello there, you must be Mrs Carter. I'm Tom Fraser, and I'm very sorry to have kept you waiting.'
Sharon follows Tom into his office. She notices that he does not sit at his desk, which is against the wall in the corner. He asks her a few questions about when she will be moving and the ages of her children (she has two, one who will be coming into the nursery and one who will be joining the reception class). He speaks briefly about what the school is trying to achieve academically and socially and gives Sharon a copy of the school brochure. Then he says:
'I think it would be best if I took you around the school and you can see for yourself what sort of place it is. We'll start in the nursery and then we'll visit the rest of the school and then perhaps I can leave you back in the nursery with Mrs Jones, our home school teacher.'
As Tom says this he hopes that Karen Jones will be back from the home visits that she is making this morning. In fact she is already on her way back; one of the children she had planned to see was ill. She has been welcomed into two homes, having rung a few days earlier to make an appointment. The two mothers have already been to an introductory meeting at the school to find out about the way the nursery works, and have taken up the offer

of a follow-up visit to their own homes. Karen has sat and chatted to them in their own environments and taken each child a present – a pack full of pencils, crayons and activities to do at home. Both the mothers have been much more talkative than they were at the meeting in school and have told Karen a lot about what their children are capable of doing and what they enjoy. They have also been able to express worries – one of them, for instance, is worried that her daughter still wets the bed at night and sometimes has accidents during the day. Karen is reassuring and explains that the nursery staff will remind her daughter about going to the toilet and will be happy to lend dry knickers. Karen has had the opportunity to talk and play with the children in their own homes and has met one of the fathers, who admitted that he had been interested in coming to the meeting at school but felt 'it would be all women'.

As she enters the school Karen stops at the secretary's office to talk to Anne and tell her a little about what a pleasant and informative morning she has had. Anne informs her about Joe Shaw's visit and that Tom is taking a new parent around the school. As Karen enters the nursery Tom and Sharon are just leaving. They have been talking to the nursery nurse and the supply teacher about the activities that the children are doing, and one of the mums who has been baking with the children has explained the workings of the toy library.

Tom and Sharon continue their trip around the school. Sharon is particularly impressed by the presence of parents in the classrooms and by the happy faces of the children working with the special needs support teacher. It seems very different from her memories of remedial reading classes. She also notices that, although the children seem to be allowed to talk and move around while they have tasks to do, there is a calm working atmosphere.

When she meets up again with Karen in the nursery, preparations are being made for lunch and Karen suggests they go and have a chat in the entrance hall. Sharon asks some questions about the school routine and talks about some concerns she has about her son, who has had difficulties at his present school. The possibility of Karen and the reception teacher visiting Sharon and the children at home, in her new house or at her mother's, is discussed.

Discussion

Well, that's the story. What you make of it will obviously depend on the various personal and professional factors which influence your immediate responses and reactions. Different readers will have different interpretations.

What, for instance, do you make of that first encounter in the head's office? Joe Shaw, the parent, is obviously distressed and his anger is initially vented in an uncontrolled manner. Is Tom's reaction that of a weak headteacher who has not defined boundaries sufficiently clearly, or an appropriate response from someone who believes Mr Shaw has something important to say and wants to help him become more coherent? What about Tom's response to the question of hitting back: is he explicitly condoning double standards in saying that Joe's advice to his children is appropriate in some circumstances, or is he acknowledging the coexistence of cultures? What about his strong statement that Joe's recommended strategy will never be allowed in school: is this the head 'coming the heavy' or a principled statement of important values that underpin the school culture and curriculum?

My purpose in asking these questions is to acknowledge ambiguities and differences of interpretation possibly attaching to this and every interaction in the story. It might perhaps be a useful exercise to interrogate all of them from two or three different perspectives. Nevertheless, the reader will remember that the purpose of the story was to present a summary of some general themes. The discussion that follows explores the themes of mutual understanding and respect, and sharing of expertise and information mentioned in the short extract from the Rumbold Report (DES 1990) at the beginning of this chapter. Alongside these important aspects of partnership, the attitudes and skills that the participants in this particular home–school partnership are developing are also implicitly examined.

If we go back again to that first incident in Tom's office, we see mutual understanding and respect manifested in various ways. Joe's initial intrusion could perhaps be seen as disrespectful, but Tom accepts it without anger and without reference to his pile of paperwork. He recognizes that Joe is feeling stressed and that the school is open not just to 'well-behaved' parents but also to those who are distressed. He wants the interaction to have a positive outcome if possible. On one occasion when I interviewed Tom he said: 'If you send negative messages you'll get a negative reaction. No matter how a parent comes through that door – they may be screaming, they may be jumping up and down, you may know there's enormous problems, that they have come here to have a row, but my first approach is always "How can I help you?"' The person-centred approach manifested in the school brochure was mentioned earlier. Tom sees himself in this situation as a skilled helper or counsellor; he is not frightened or intimidated by Joe's behaviour, he merely sees it as inappropriately aggressive and he therefore counters it with what Carl Rogers (1951) referred to as 'unconditional positive regard'. This is important for somebody who is as lacking in self-esteem as Tom understands Joe is. A refusal to be deflected by defensive behaviour and be drawn into the expected row breaks into the negative self-defeating cycle which Joe has set up for himself and offers acceptance of his intrinsic worth. Joe can then become more coherent about his concerns.

Tom responds to the question of hitting back with a reference to the principle of respect. Joe no longer responds angrily and indeed listens carefully, but the two men agree to differ in their approaches to physical violence. They have both had their ideas acknowledged and respected. This incident manifestly raises questions about the possible conflicts involved between school and home culture. These are inevitable whatever the perceived social class, ethnic origin, gender or sexual orientation of both parents and staff. They may be more obvious or assume more immediate importance in some areas but, as many teachers know, parents are aware that home and school represent two different worlds for their children, simply from listening to them talk and observing their behaviour. This area will be returned to in subsequent discussion of issues around conflict and boundary-setting.

Sharon Carter, the new parent, is also treated with respect and understanding before she has even spoken to anybody in the building. Her needs have been considered by staff, she is able to find her way in without embarrassment or difficulty. The school secretary knows that she will be arriving, is able to greet her appropriately and reassuringly, and shows no hesitation in putting Sharon's comfort before her own work for a few minutes. The hall where Sharon waits is comfortable – yet more evidence that staff have thought about the needs of visitors. There is also plenty of information about the school on show. Like every other educational establishment, Queens Road receives a lot of visitors of various sorts – parents and other members of the local community, LEA advisers, professionals from outside agencies (social workers, speech therapists, health visitors, educational psychologists, for example), salespeople, college tutors and students to name but a few. Anyone who is waiting there can find out about many aspects of school life – the school's history, its aims, the curriculum offered, activities recently undertaken outside school, community events and so on. Children's work, photographs and writing are displayed in a series of matching frames that look professional and can be more easily and quickly assembled than the traditional display board. The staff at Queens Road are proud of their school and the children they teach; they also recognize the importance of marketing, of creating a good impression. They know that one of the most common ways for people to gain information about a place is through networking and gossip; that people from all the groups mentioned above talk to each other about the places they visit.

If this had been written ten years ago I doubt whether 'marketing' would have seemed an appropriate terminology, However, the legislation of the last few years has led to shifts in both power and language. There is not space here to explore the ideology of the New Right's attitudes to parents and educators as embodied in the Parents' Charter and the Education Acts of 1980, 1981, 1986, 1988 and 1992. It must not, however, be forgotten that parental involvement is a political issue and, like the curriculum, no longer an individual establishment issue. Beresford (1992: 53) writes as a home school teacher about both the general effects of such legislation on teachers and parents and the particular ways in which it has affected her own practice. She talks about the 'dilemma of the ethical entrepreneur' when it comes to selling the school, and the danger that 'perceiving the parent primarily as a "consumer" in a marketplace could lead to the involvement of parents becoming a superficial public relations exercise rather than a meaningful educational partnership'. In other words, there may be a risk of emphasizing what Bastiani (1988) characterizes as an 'accountability' model of parental involvement rather than the other two models which he identifies, namely 'communication' and 'participation'. At Queens Road the meaningful educational partnership underpins the public relations and, although accountability is acknowledged as important, communication and participation are paramount.

Indeed, a lot of verbal communication goes on during our story. Children and parents are listened to and allowed space; staff talk does not dominate. Children talk to Sharon while she is waiting in the hall; Emma talks easily to the head and enjoys a joke with him; parents talk to a member of staff about what they have been doing that morning; the same parents talk to Sharon; Sharon notices the children throughout the school talking to each other and to nursery nurses, teachers and parents; Karen, the home school teacher, visits parents at home to chat. There is plenty of what the Rumbold Report described as 'sharing expertise and information'. All these interactions are characterized by friendliness and an assumption that all participants have something interesting and useful to say. Sharon probably noticed evidence of all the criteria for making choices about starting school listed by Hale (1992). The caring, relaxed atmosphere has been built upon mutual respect and high expectations of everybody. As Jackie says to Sharon: 'The staff are nice, they've always been all right with me – if they're all right with you, then you're all right with them.' Jane sums up staff attitudes when she says: 'they're not looking at you every minute and you feel like you belong.'

At Queens Road, as in most establishments, the staff emphasize the importance of links with parents before the children start in the nursery. They recognize the importance of parents' roles as their children's first educators and they understand 'the factors affecting ease of transition and continuity of experience' (DES 1990: 47). Karen's home visiting programme is an explicit acknowledgement of these understandings. She knows that many new children will greet her on their first day in nursery with 'You came to my house', that their parents will have experienced her as a warm, friendly non-patronizing visitor who is prepared to leave school territory and who is interested in them and their views about their children.

As well as being the nursery teacher, Karen also has responsibility for home–school links generally. Her role involves working with and supporting other staff (although it is important to realize that at Queens Road all staff are expected to prioritize relationships with parents) and she is always keen to help parents become involved in the life of the school. Karen's role is perceived as encouraging mutual understanding. Parents like Jackie who perhaps start by helping in the nursery, where they are known and feel confident, are then encouraged to get to know other staff and older children. As Jackie says to Sharon: 'I know more about how the school works and I see more than the nursery in action. I know where Kelly will be in the future.' At Queens Road, therefore, parents have opportunities to experience the life of the whole school from the first day of their child's school experience rather than 'moving up' with their children.

The possibility of conflict and clash of cultures was mentioned earlier in connection with Joe Shaw's views on discipline. Although a climate of mutual dialogue and understanding is obviously present at Queens Road it did not occur as if by magic; various decisions about boundaries have been made and ground rules established. Pollard (1985: 28) talks about the potential threat to teacher autonomy posed by parents:

> the structural source of the problem here is that, while parents are concerned for their particular child, the teacher has responsibility for all the children in the class. Furthermore given the resources available, teachers cannot always provide the quality of education which they might like. They are thus vulnerable to parents who wish to make specific observations or complaints or to question policies. The fact that parents are likely to know a lot more than the teacher about many aspects of their child in a sense only aggravates the problem.

The wishes and needs of staff and parents often have to be balanced sensitively as they may not always be in harmony. When Jackie and Jane, for instance, first appear in the story they are talking with a member of staff. She goes into the staffroom and they remain in the hall. The staff have decided that they do not wish parents to use the staffroom – it is a fairly small room and they feel the need to have one place where they can relax away from both children and parents. Staff always make sure, however, that any parents in school get a drink when they do. In the story Emma talks about taking drinks to parents.

Joe Shaw goes to the headteacher with his complaint about his son's treatment at the hands of one of the teachers. This behaviour accords with the system that has been worked out over the years and which is designed to prevent distressed or angry parents exploding into the classrooms – it is better for them, their children and the staff if they are able to let off steam first if necessary. The headteacher is more likely to be able to give them undivided attention than a busy nursery nurse or teacher whose first responsibility must be to the children in the class. Tom does suggest to Joe, however, that the next step should be for him to talk to Wayne's class teacher. He wants to get them talking to each other.

Just as the parents are expected to respect the staff's rights and needs, so we see Karen, the home school teacher, setting up home visits in a way which presents the parents with choice. All the prospective nursery parents are asked to a meeting at school and then given the option of a visit. Most of them are glad to take this up but some prefer not to; nobody is confronted with an unexpected visit. There is an important crossing of normal boundaries involved in home visits, one that may be difficult for both parties. Karen herself, who is a very experienced teacher with a longstanding commitment to working with parents, has admitted to being 'very nervous' when she first began doing them.

The fact that this is a working-class area, where many families have social and financial problems, does not deter the staff and governors from having high expectations of the children and their parents. The reference in the first paragraph of the story to the two children who had to come in through the front door because of lateness exemplifies the staff's refusal to compromise on what they see as an important issue. One of Tom's beliefs is that 'We mustn't give these kids a second-class education'. To him that means offering the children the best education the staff can and being prepared to 'beg, borrow and steal' to get resources and funding. It also means expecting and getting a commitment from the parents to what the school is trying to do for the children. The lateness issue is an example. So many children were arriving late for school that the staff reckoned that many were not receiving their full entitlement to a good education and the beginning of the day was unnecessarily difficult to manage. They decided to bolt classroom doors shortly after the official start of the school day and thus force all latecomers to use the front door and report to the secretary. Some parents objected strongly to this, but the result is that very few children are late and school starts for everyone when it is supposed to.

The special needs support referred to in the story is an example of the school taking action on behalf of the children. Some years ago the staff were worried by the low reading attainment of some of the children. The school now employs two support teachers on a job-share basis and the reading scores are better than average. These teachers work closely with class teachers and parents and take withdrawal groups for intensive work to help them catch up with their peers. They can monitor and assess the children's skills and needs very closely.

Another area in which Queens Road is successful is in getting parents to attend parents' evenings. There are three a year and the aim is to see every child's parents at least once. In 1992–3 only one child's parents were not seen at all. All formal events are combined with some opportunity for socializing such as free wine and cheese or tea and coffee, videos of children in action and plenty of staff around to talk to. It is made clear to parents that they are expected to attend by the way in which staff personally and informally follow up non-attenders and base their conversation or correspondence around the presumption that parents are interested in their children's education.

Tom is pleased by the level of interest shown by the parents in the school and claims that, although there has sometimes been conflict about issues such as lateness, the way in which he and the staff have stuck to their principles has earned them the respect of the vast majority of the parents. He says that they now know that arguments about issues of principle take place because the staff care about the children's education and not because they are awkward or 'teachery'.

There are many more issues arising from the story of that Thursday morning at Queens Road Primary School that could be discussed and analysed. Whatever your personal conclusions at this stage, I hope you feel that it was a story about a group of people who are committed to making their relationships work for the benefit of the children, and I hope your own thinking and possible future practice have been challenged in some way by your reading. The questions which follow are designed to be used in conjunction with the story and for the purposes of reviewing current workplace practice.

Questions for discussion

1 What interpersonal skills do staff working with parents need to develop?

2 The Introduction to this book sets out a list of summary statements about the knowledge, skills and attitudes that adults working with the under-fives and their families should possess (DES 1990: 47). How evident are these both in the story and in your workplace?

3 What else would you like to know about Queens Road School or the local community?

4 At present Queens Road serves a mainly white community, but the ethnic balance may shift in the near future. What are the implications for future work with parents?

5 What are your thoughts about the father who told Karen that he would have liked to attend the nursery meeting but he was afraid 'it would be all women'?

6 How welcoming is your workplace to parents and other visitors? How do you know?

7 What do your establishment's written communications with parents look like? What sort of response do they receive?

8 What strategies do you use to enable participation in your workplace from the maximum number of parents and carers?

9 How do you ensure that issues of confidentiality are understood by everybody involved?

10 The Rumbold Report and many others use the word 'partnership' to describe the ideal relationship with parents. Is that an accurate description, or are you striving for some other sort of relationship?

Further reading

Atkin, J. and Bastiani, J. (1988) *Listening to Parents: An Approach to the Improvement of Home–School Relations.* London: Cassell.

Bastiani, J. (1989) *Working with Parents: A Whole School Approach.* Windsor, NFER/Nelson.

Edwards, V. and Redfern A. (1988) *At Home in School.* London: Routledge.

Wolfendale, S. (1992) *Empowering Parents and Teachers: Working for Children.* London: Cassell.

Woodhead, M. and McGrath A. (eds) (1988) *Family, School and Society.* London: Hodder & Stoughton.

9

'Look at me – I'm only two': Educare for under-threes: The importance of early experience

Brenda Griffin

> The period from birth to five is one of rapid growth and development, both physical and intellectual. At this stage children's developmental needs are complex and interrelated.
>
> (DES 1990: 7)

Child-care workers from a variety of professional backgrounds and disciplincs, as wcll as parcnts, have a significant role to play in the development of young children. As Wilson (1978: 25) states:

> essentially a biological organism whose main concern is with maintaining its physical comfort, the human infant develops into a fully fledged individual with a unique set of values, attributes, aspirations, tendencies and characteristic ways of perceiving and responding to the world and to himself [*sic*].

The importance for the early years professional in acquiring the knowledge and skills needed to understand and respond to the needs of very young children cannot be overestimated. This chapter will explore some of the experiences of our youngest children in day-care settings and, through the case study presented, consider evidence which may contribute to identifying quality childhood experience.

I use the term 'educare' to refer to the holistic experience of care and education for children under three in day-care settings (see also Chapter 5). The term is commonly used in Europe, is referred to by David (1990) and further explored by Calder (1990b), who claims that care can too often conjure up custodial images and that educare should encompass care, education and enjoyment. In the UK there is a history of provision for very young children being a private matter between individuals, with little support from local or central government:

> the main form of care for children under the age of three is that given by relatives, followed by childminders and a long way behind, nurseries and nannies ... In addition surveys show a substantial number of two year olds in playgroups.
>
> (Hennessy *et al.* 1992: 8)

The under-threes may be found in a wide range of establishment-based settings, as indicated by the Rumbold Committee (DES 1990: 2). Under the broad title of 'nursery' we can find: local authority day nurseries which give places to children from families who can demonstrate the greatest need; private nurseries with places given to those who can pay (this is an increasing form of provision, especially in those areas with little local authority provision); workplace nurseries offering day-care facilities for the children of employees; local educational authority nursery schools and classes which provide free education for children between three and five years; and combined nursery centres which integrate day care and nursery facilities in a single unit, again usually providing for the children of families demonstrating the greatest need. Ferri *et al.* (1981: 132) offer an early overview of combined provision and suggest that the following features are essential:

- good physical care;   *but no curriculum.*
- appropriate emotional care, including a close emotional relationship with the same adult;
- a secure familiar home base providing for comfort and rest away from the main stream of group activities;
- activities which stimulate intellectual development, including verbal interaction with adults on a one-to-one basis.

This diversity of provision would be welcomed if it offered real choice to families; however, there is much evidence that this is not so, and, as Pugh (1992) points out, there has always been a tension between professionally defined need and consumer demand. The Rumbold Report urges 'those who make provision to recognise the extent to which demand outstrips supply and to secure a continuing expansion of high quality services to meet children's and their parents needs' (DES 1990: 1). Criteria for admission varies considerably between establishments, whether it be 'children in need' as defined by the Children Act 1989 or the financial cost incurred by the economy-led private sector. There are, of course, many areas of the UK which lack any of these services. The National Commission (1993) emphasizes the detrimental effects on children and families of this omission. Access is frequently prevented by the limited supply set against the demand for some form of provision.

The 1990s have brought major demographic changes. There has been a significant reduction in the number of young people entering the job market and a major increase in the number of women with young children entering it. These increases are likely to continue over the next decade, with a key issue being the increased demand for some form of day care. The recent introduction of a modernized registration system (Children Act 1989) provides local authorities with an opportunity to look critically at the way in which they exercise their regulatory function. We could be optimistic that this protection will safeguard the quality of experience for young children in day care, but what is *quality experience* and how can it be measured? The Rumbold Report (DES 1990) made a series of recommendations to assist in the identification of quality provision and was welcomed by a huge number of early years workers, many of whom could identify with the importance and relevance of this document for their work. Another discussion paper focusing on quality is that produced by the European Commission Childcare Network which suggests that 'the process of defining quality is important in its own right, providing the opportunity for values, ideas, knowledge and experience to be shared examined and better understood' (Balageur et al. 1992: 5). The paper is intended to be a resource for that purpose and offers criteria in the forms of questions to be addressed in a number of areas, some of which are highlighted in Chapters 1 and 7 of this book. Hennessy et al. (1992) considered the findings of various research projects in several countries, together with their own involvement in a major longitudinal study of British day care for children. They suggest there are certain features which need to exist in order to facilitate quality experience for very young children. Some of these are:

- warmth, affection and consistency towards the children;
- lots of communication, with the adults being responsive to the children;
- learning opportunities to improve the basic knowledge of children about the world and provide them with new skills;
- developmentally appropriate experiences which change as children develop;
- the nurturing of children's talent for self-initiated learning and of curiosity about the world;
- consistent and responsive relationships;
- attachments to several care givers;
- opportunities for interaction with other children.

In my attempt to identify the indicators of quality experiences for children under three years, I spent some time in both participant and non-participant observation of children and carers in a combined nursery centre. The following are some of the questions I asked. What were the children enjoying or not enjoying? To what kind of resources did they have access? Who makes decisions about access to equipment? What responses were children getting from each other and from the adults around them? Who initiates play? How are disputes handled? What are the children's views about their experience?

About Suzie

The following is an account of what happened to Suzie, aged two years nine months, and some of her friends over a two-hour period one morning in May 1993. I arrived at the nursery at 9.30 and was welcomed by the staff team. Immediately some of the children came to draw me into their play. I sat with them and observed Suzie from a distance as she was playing in the sand while at the same time holding tightly on to a rag doll belonging to the nursery. She left one hand free to enjoy the texture and to explore the properties and possibilities of the sand as she talked and occasionally sang to the doll. There were several other children playing in the sand and one adult worker who talked with the children as they played. Suzie made no attempt to be involved in the conversation, nor did she respond when the adult attempted to include her. At one point Suzie needed both hands to succeed in scooping sand into a container but was unwilling to put the doll down. She solved the problem by attempting to use one of the doll's arms as a second hand. Suzie experienced some success with this, but when another, bigger child came along and tried to squeeze into a small space alongside her it was clear that Suzie was thinking about her situation and what to do about it. There was enough room if Suzie would put down the doll, but she wanted the doll to be involved. Her decision was made quickly and she moved away from the sand tray into the book area, where she selected a book and sat on a large floor cushion and proceeded to tell a story from the book to her doll.

Approximately ten minutes later Suzie, still engrossed in a second book and the doll on her knee, was joined by an adult who was Suzie's key worker. She sat alongside Suzie with her own book and began to read silently. Suzie was not distracted at first, but when she had finished her book she replaced it on the shelf, placed herself on the knee of the adult, had a brief cuddle, then asked to be read to. The adult's response was warm and encouraging, and Suzie sat in this way for fifteen minutes and enjoyed three stories and many cuddles. In between reading the adult talked to Suzie about what might happen next in the story, relating events in the book to Suzie's experience and to the nursery environment. At one point drinks were served to the children but Suzie clearly did not want to leave the situation. This was quite acceptable to the adult.

Eventually Suzie had tired of books and moved across the nursery to an area where several children were building with large bricks. Sitting on the perimeter for a while and clearly enjoying being an observer, she then decided to play. There were enough bricks for all the children and Suzie was able to join in and put her ideas into practice. At first she appeared to be playing with colour; as her tower grew it had a distinct pattern to it. The adult at the centre of the play commented upon this, but Suzie chose to ignore her and concentrate on her tower which was growing in terms of size, shape and colour. Suzie seemed pleased with her efforts, and again the adult commented on her achievements. This time Suzie responded: 'It's big.' The adult was aware that Suzie was pleased and while her comments were positive and her responses appropriate she saw no need to encourage her further because the self-satisfaction Suzie showed was sufficient.

Suzie then moved away to the home corner, where an adult and three other children were playing. The adult, helped by the children, was changing the doll's bed linen and collecting dolls' clothes and the like to take to the laundry. Suzie joined in the task, holding on to the doll and refusing, when requested by one of the other children, to undress it. She helped collect the clothes and take them to the laundry room, where the adult allowed the children to load and set the washing machine. The adult talked to the children about who washed their clothes and with what. She talked about what might happen when the clothes were ready, encouraging the children to predict and recall. Eventually they all returned to the home corner and pretended to clean the furniture using hand towels from the bathroom. Recognizing and responding to their evident interest, the adult supplied materials so that the children could clean the furniture for real! Suzie stayed with this activity for ten minutes, fully concentrating on the task in hand. When she did move away it was to take a pram; carefully placing her doll inside it, she pushed it through the nursery, negotiating her way between adults and activities out to the garden. She walked towards the first adult who was bending down on the grass with a small group of children collecting fallen twigs and leaves. Suzie joined them at the invitation of the adult who explained what was happening. The adult was Suzie's key worker, the same person who had read to her earlier in the day. Her responses to all the children were warm and encouraging, and at Suzie's request she gave both her doll and her a cuddle. Suzie placed the doll in the arms of the adult, then, replacing her in the pram, she returned inside. Suzie had held on to the doll all morning, finding a way to build, read, play with sand and later have a snack without relinquishing her hold.

I continued to watch Suzie that morning. Her play, although solitary, was rich in experience and supported by the adults around her. She solved problems, made decisions and shared experiences with her doll. It was evident she enjoyed the freedom to choose her own activity and showed confidence in her surroundings, moving freely around the nursery, spending between ten and fifteen minutes in any one area and returning to favourites on several occasions. During this time her play was entirely of her own choosing. What are the quality issues in Suzie's experience? In beginning to analyse the experiences Suzie had that morning, I am reminded of the words of Rouse and Griffin (1992: 156), who suggest that 'an ethos of respect for and dignity in childhood may be set from the cradle' and that 'quality educare is apparent in the strong attachments between adults and children'.

About the nursery

The nursery admits children from two to four years of age, with the possibility on occasion for much younger children to be admitted, although this is usually under emergency circumstances. The 'key worker' system in operation (Cowley 1991) gives each child and family one very special person to whom they will relate. That person will be responsible for establishing a close relationship with a group of up to six children, developing, in collaboration with the children's parents/carers, a curriculum unique to each child. In this establishment the curriculum seeks to address the following principles:

- all the opportunities for learning and development that are made available for children;
- the activities, attitudes and behaviour that are planned, encouraged, tolerated, ignored or forbidden;
- the way in which the room is organized, and the routines followed by the children and adults;
- the part adults take in organizing, directing, influencing and joining in what the children do;
- the extent to which parents are involved in the above.

An important question in examining any provision for young children, and in particular that in the case study presented in this chapter, is the degree to which these issues are addressed.

Calder (1990b: 23) reminds us that:

The distinctive nature of the curriculum for the under threes should be focussed upon the happiness of the child. This is what loving parents want for their children and we need theories that can integrate both the affective and cognitive.

The nursery is organized so that children who are under three have a place of their own, although all children do have access to all areas. The area for under-threes is light, airy and spacious and the staff team have created distinctive 'corners' for play. There is a separate area for activities such as paint, sand and water and a mark-making area with a table on which the children can write. A large 'soft' area plays a significant role in the children's day and my observations confirmed my belief that very young children spend a high proportion of time in this place. It contains a large comfortable settee, cushions of various sizes covered in fabrics of different colours and textures, a fitted carpet and rugs, and soft, round play materials made of natural substances which are stored in cardboard containers. All the resources are available to the smallest child, signalling that this is a place where there is no need to ask for help or to be told 'no', 'stop' or 'don't'.

The organization of the nursery and the sensitive responses of the adults ensured that Suzie's individual needs were met and that she had some control of her own learning. The way materials were presented drew Suzie to them. Ease of access to resources enabled Suzie to make choices and help herself. She was not bombarded with questions, which less aware adults find hard to resist, but encouraged to take part in meaningful discussion with the adults who talked through what she was doing. Her reluctance to 'talk back' was respected. The adults did not intrude into Suzie's play, but they did respond to it. The planning of the nursery environment had minimized the need for children to be dependent on adults, and positively encouraged them to be independent. Much thought had gone into the accessibility of equipment and to the provision of situations where children might be dependent upon the co-operation of others. In this nursery all the 'art work' on display belongs to the children completely, there are no pre-cut shapes for children to fill in and all the children are encouraged, by the provision of materials and the sensitive interaction of the adults, to experiment with textures and substances without the pressure of the demand for a finished product. This supports the view of the Rumbold Committee (DES 1990: 9) that:

For the early years educator, therefore, the process of education – how children learn – is as important as, and inseparable from, the content – what they learn. We believe that this principle must underlie all curriculum planning for the under fives.

The children's work is respected, valued, discussed and enjoyed with the child, and what happens to it is the result of this discussion. It may be taken home, placed in the child's personal box or displayed in the nursery. There is no 'adult agenda' for what has been created by the children.

The nursery is able to offer choice to children, allowing them to engage in decision-making processes. Access to outdoor play is available throughout sessions, so where the learning experiences take place is up to the child. Young children need to explore and experiment in a variety of environments and on different surfaces. This belief was reinforced for me on my first visit to Romania soon after the revolution. I was working in a hospital with children, some as old as six, who had spent most of their lives in a cot. One sunny afternoon a colleague and I decided to take four of the children to the park which was adjacent to the hospital. The terror for the children began as soon as we went through the hospital door. Because they had lived all of their lives in this institution they had never before stepped upon an uneven surface or experienced so much space, they had never felt the wind on their faces or heard the sounds of traffic and birds and rustling trees. Our attempt at giving four children a happy visit to the park had become a nightmare for us all.

Young children must be safe, and their safety is the responsibility of adults. They must be given opportunities to express freely their ideas, emotions and theories. They must also be secure if they are to have the confidence to move around, develop, test and practice skills, if they are to have new experiences which will aid their understanding of the world, if they are to learn of the boundaries, the limitations and the wonderful possibilities of what they *can do*.

In discussion with the key worker I was able to find out more about Suzie's behaviour that day. Suzie has two parents. Her mother was in hospital at the time of my observation and, in an attempt to help Suzie understand this, a structured play area was set up in the form of a hospital in the nursery as one of the many activities from which she could select. As Suzie was reading to her doll her key worker decided that it was appropriate to join her but without disturbing her. She sat in the book area reading one of the books from the local library about hospitalization. Suzie responded well to this opportunity to understand more about what was happening in her life and, of course, to take some emotional strength from the significant person in this environment, hence the cuddle. The appropriateness of the adult's actions gave Suzie support at a difficult time. The adult made herself available, she was using Suzie's demonstrated interests to meet her needs and this was clearly welcomed by her. Suzie had been treated with respect. The key worker further explained that Suzie had commandeered the doll at about the time her mother had been admitted to hospital. There had been occasions when other children would have liked it but Suzie refused to put it down, her need for the doll at this time being greater than that of the other children.

There was evidence in the nursery that the children could understand the needs of others. Bruce (1987) considers this point at some length when discussing the work of Piaget (1968) which led early childhood workers to take the view that young children were unable to look at situations from another child's view. She points out:

> one can think of many situations which did not quite fit in with this blanket view that the child was 'egocentric' until five years. For example, four year old Wally had been unhappy when settling into school himself. He took three year old Peter by the hand and cuddled him when he saw that he was about to cry on his first day. He knew what it was like to be 'new' and could empathise.
>
> (Bruce 1987: 134)

I recall an experience of my own from some years ago when I had two 13-month-old children on my knee while watching a nursery concert. One of the children began to cry, and the other bent forward and across to reach the crying child. She stretched out her arms and enveloped the crying child, gently patting her back and making the sound 'Ahh'. She recognized the unhappiness and recalled an appropriate response. After several minutes the two

were stroking, cooing and cuddling each other, a precious moment
for me and an early learning experience for the children. If two
13-month-old babies could empathize then it was possible for
Suzie's friends to do so, too.

The adults

The sensitivity and appropriateness of adult interactions with children is vital at all stages of their development.

Adults have the power to make a major difference to children's lives and their development by what they offer to
children and by how they behave towards them. They have a
responsibility to help children through more difficult phases
and support them in dealing with experiences that threaten
their development or well being.

(Linden 1993: 75)

The Rumbold Committee (DES 1990: 1) was firm in its belief
about the importance of the adult: 'we believe it to be vital that
all who work, or are involved, with young children recognise the
importance of their educational role and fulfil it'. The knowledge,
understanding and skills required of adults working with very young
children is explored elsewhere in this book, specifically in Chapter
7. Sensitivity to young children's needs and potential is required
in order to create an appropriate and individual curriculum for
each child. Hennessy *et al.* (1992) examine closely the behaviour
of care givers and educators and their effects on children's development in Britain, France, Denmark and the USA, and signal the
benefits for young children from the provision of developmentally
appropriate learning experiences and opportunities.

It is important that we remember that preoccupation with what
children should be doing at two, three and four years of age can
cause us to miss the achievements of what they are doing successfully and confidently now. I firmly believe that if a child has not
been allowed to be 'properly' two then he/she will not be properly
three or four or five! The adult in the case study was aware of the
importance of celebrating each child's achievement and not com-
pelled to measure this against some predetermined scale. Piaget's
influence on educational research and his emphasis on the match

or mismatch between levels of understanding in children's learning using a 'top-down' model can suggest failure to achieve, whereas Isaacs's 'bottom-up' perspective concentrates on current competences (Athey 1990). The highly trained and sensitive adult in the case study spent time in which she observed Suzie, discovered her interests, recognized her level of development, had some knowledge of the child's world and offered the appropriate challenge, support materials, environment and opportunity to succeed.

The older (more mature) the child, the greater the possibility that the curriculum will be group-orientated. The National Curriculum has the expectation that Key Stage 1 children (five to seven) will achieve within a range of levels. Some children in nursery settings may be feeling the effects of downward pressure, and some of those children may be as young as three years. This may be seen in establishments where staff are inappropriately trained or have limited access to professional development. Adults who are caring for and educating young children will need to be strong to resist this pressure.

Hennessy et al. (1992), in identifying principles for potential quality, believe that the ratio of adults to children must reflect the stage of development and the time required by the adult to respond appropriately. The curriculum offered should be more than a watered down version of what is on offer to older children and reflect the interest and abilities of each child. When considering the quality of experience for very young children in day-care settings we must at all times be mindful of the criteria of quality held by children themselves. Katz (1993: 7) suggests that we might put ourselves in the place of a child and ask:

- Do I usually feel welcome rather than trapped?
- Do I belong rather than just function as one of a crowd?
- Am I usually accepted and understood rather than overlooked or scolded by the adults?
- Am I usually addressed seriously and respectfully, rather than as precious or cute?
- Am I usually accepted by some of my peers, rather than isolated, or rejected by them?
- Are most of the activities interesting rather than frivolous or boring?

- Are most of the activities meaningful rather than trivial or mindless?
- Are most of the activities engaging and absorbing, rather than just amusing, fun, entertaining or exciting?
- Am I usually glad to be here, rather than eager to leave?

We may well be surprised and disturbed by some of the answers! Further questions which might be useful for staff discussion and in raising awareness of the ways in which the earliest experiences of young children can be enriched, might include the following:

- How far is the provision encouraging independence/dependence?
- How much respect/disrespect is shown to children?
- How much of what children do or wish to do is valued/devalued?
- How far have we organized our space and resources to cater for the individual child?
- How much value do we place on close relationships with children and their families?
- How far do we draw on the knowledge and skills of others to fulfil our obligations to children?
- How much control are we willing to relinquish?
- How far are we enabling/disabling children?

In responding to these and other questions drawn from Suzie's experiences we may move a little closer to the 'quality early experience' which we owe to our youngest children.

Suzie revisited

Suzie's life had been disrupted by her mother's hospitalization, and she had to come to terms with this in a two-year-old way. Life is like that for most children because things happen and change occurs. Having to spend a large part of her waking hours in the world of the nursery where enlightened adults are making appropriate provision in a supportive environment, Suzie and her friends will be helped to deal with this reality in a positive and enriching way.

Soon Suzie and her friends will be three-year-olds, and what will adults expect of them then? Fortunately in Suzie's case she will be 'properly three' because she has been allowed and encouraged to be 'properly two'!

Further reading

Cowley L. (1991) *Young Children in Group Day Care*. London: National Children's Bureau.

Hennessy, E., Martin, S., Moss, P. and Melhuish, E. (1992) *Children and Day Care: Lessons from Research*. London: Paul Chapman.

Pugh, G. (ed.) (1992) *Contemporary Issues in the Early Years – Working Collaboratively for Children*. London: Paul Chapman.

Rouse, D. (1990) *Babies and Toddlers Carers and Educators – Quality for Under 3s*. London: National Children's Bureau.

Looking to the future: Concluding comments

Lesley Abbott

In presenting a range of case studies in which children and adults have been variously working and playing, talking and communicating, learning and laughing, caring and sharing, we have identified what for us have been quality encounters with each other, with the curriculum, and with the wider community. At no time has it been our intention to present dichotomies or to polarize approaches or methods of educating young children. As Webb (1972: 15) reminds us in relation to the work–play debate:

> It does not matter whether a child is said to be playing or working so much as whether the activity is of a kind that, in one way or another, is promoting further mastery – whether that mastery is of himself or herself, the environment, mother-tongue, simple skills or complex concepts ... what we may choose to *label* the activity should cease to engage so much of our time.

We would claim that the children and adults in these case studies were involved in mastery of one kind or another – be it of themselves, or of skills, concepts, knowledge, values, attitudes or experience. We have evidence of parents in relationships with sensitive educators being 'empowered', gaining confidence and skill in taking their rightful place in the education process.

The Royal Society of the Arts Enquiry, *Start Right* (RSA 1994), begins with the premise that 'teachers are important, parents are fundamental'. In every chapter parents have played an important role – in talking, playing, assessing, teaching and learning along-side their children and those responsible for their care and education in the establishments visited. The chapters which have focused specifically on parents and the quality of the partnerships and relationships between them and their children's educators highlight the need for sensitivity and respect on both sides. Asked to pinpoint what, for her, were the essential issues in her chapter, Helen Strahan concludes:

> I guess the major message of my chapter is that, although any establishment can come up with lots of good ideas for working with parents, the most important issue is attitudes and values. These influence the quality of relationships more powerfully than anything else. (It's no good putting up 'welcome to our school' signs all over the place if people do not behave in a welcoming manner when you get there.) There are some fundamental areas that need to be considered by the whole staff, such as creating an ethos based on mutual respect and understanding. This cannot have a chance of being established if the head does not treat the staff with respect – strong leadership based on strong principles seems important in the story. Parents will not be respected and valued if children aren't. The ethos will determine how difficult issues such as conflicts of culture and expectation are dealt with and how mutually agreed ground rules emerge. I think the school in my story sees parents as both clients, customers and partners – they don't think that the relationship can be summed up solely as partnership. In other words, working with parents is as complex a job as teaching their children.

Chris Marsh, having spent many hours talking with parents, and Janice Adams, seeking their views on their involvement in policy-making, agree with Pugh and De'Ath (1989) that:

> The key question is not, how many parents can be persuaded to help, but the basis of the relationship between parents and the 'professional' educators. *Real* partnership demands a shared sense of purpose, mutual respect and a willingness to negotiate. It requires open, regular and reciprocal communication, where achievements are celebrated, problems confronted, solutions sought, and policies implemented *jointly and*

together. It takes time and effort and trust. It implies that parental competence is equivalent to professional expertise.

The development of these kinds of relationships must surely be our aim for the future. Curriculum is dealt with in various ways throughout this book – implicitly in terms of everything that is happening within the establishments visited and explicitly in a case study which raises questions about the appropriateness of National Curriculum requirements determining both planning and assessment. It is encouraging that the key issues for the future identified by the National Commission (1993: 132) include:

> a curriculum for 3 and 4 year olds which should be broadly defined and not unduly prescriptive . . . By 'Curriculum' we do not imply an excessively formal school-based programme, but one which is geared to the needs of young children and emphasises first-hand experience and the central role of play and talk in learning and development.

There are echoes here of the Rumbold Report (DES 1990) and a heartening affirmation of the centrality of play in young children's learning. The overriding message coming from Brenda Griffin's chapter on a curriculum for the under-threes is that quality is about respect for children as people, and adults not having their own agendas. It is saying that children are important so let us look at these little beings and see what they are telling us. 'Look at me, I'm a person, too!' is the message from children in Sylvia Phillips's and Caroline Barratt-Pugh's chapters and should be worn as a badge by all young children. Ensuring that adults get the message and respond appropriately should be another major goal for the future!

An important strand which runs through each chapter relates to the relationship between the quality of the experiences described and analysed and the understanding and skill of the educator. In all the settings described, those responsible for the organization, planning, assessment and partnerships had received appropriate early years training, whether as a nursery nurse in a day-care setting or as an early years teacher in a nursery school or infant class.

There is no doubt that in looking to the future, the training needs of those responsible for the care and education of young children is a key issue. The Rumbold Report highlights the need for an increase in joint training, and it is encouraging that more multidisciplinary courses are now available which provide opportunities for those involved in child health, care and education to come together. It is important that these developments continue. The introduction of multidisciplinary courses, at degree level, not only provides opportunities for raising the status of early years workers in *all* establishments, but signals that high-level qualifications are necessary for all in positions of leadership and management. Curtis and Hevey (1992: 210) remind us that:

> There is no doubt that at present we are at a crossroads in training and qualifications for workers in the early years field. There is a distinct shortage of personnel with sufficient knowledge of the educational needs of young children and with the breadth of competence to fulfil emerging multidisciplinary roles, yet demand is increasing for early years workers in all types of early years provision ... it is urgent that there is a radical re-think of the content and structure of training and qualifications for early years professionals.

While arguing strongly for multiprofessional developments, the Rumbold Report highlights the need to safeguard the 'rigour and relevance of early years teacher training courses'. The focus of much attention and debate in recent times on the importance of the graduate status of early years teachers, signals the demands and complexity of the task and recognizes the high level of skill and understanding required. The report of the National Commission (1993), *Learning to Succeed*, reiterates these views and re-emphasizes the need for 'a good start' in education and for 'access and availability' to be ensured not only with regard to teacher training, but in respect of high-quality, appropriately staffed provision for all young children.

In looking to the future we are reminded by Dowling (1992) that developments in the early years are often 'an interesting mix of depressing regression and exciting development'.

Re-reading Margaret McMillan's (1930) visionary plea for quality early education, her claim that 'not merely a few children here and there, but hundreds of thousands are in dire need of education and nurture in the first years; for lack of this early succour all the rest of life is clouded and weakened' still rings true today. The recently published study, *Poverty and Inequality in the UK. The*

Effects on Children (Kumar 1993), is dedicated to 'the millions of poverty stricken children in this country whose voice is too amorphous and diffused to be heard by the powers that be'. Early childhood education owes a great deal to the pioneering spirit of Margaret McMillan and others like her.

Young children need strong advocates. Fortunately there are many still around. The National Commission presents targets for improvement and recommends that within five years nursery education must meet nationally agreed standards, that by the end of the 1990s every local authority must cater for 60 per cent of all three- and four-year-olds, and that within five years thereafter 95 per cent of four-year-olds and 85 per cent of three-year-olds should be catered for. Quality early education is the aim of the RSA (1994) report, which advocates a national target that: 'No child born [in the UK] after the year 2000 should be deprived of opportunity and support for effective early learning'.

Throughout this book we have aimed to share what we believe have been examples of quality in a range of areas. We believe that the achievement of high standards of care and education is the entitlement of every young child. The areas on which we have focused are policy, planning, practice, provision and partnership. The extent to which quality in each of these areas continues to be addressed still depends, as Webb (1972: 182) reminds us:

> not on government policy – which is ephemeral – purpose built schools or even money . . . what is decisive in determining whether children are indoctrinated into conformity, given simple custodial care, or receive a liberal education is the quality of the educators.

Bibliography

Abbott, L. (1993) 'A Study of Perceptions of Play'. Unpublished study. The Manchester Metropolitan University.

Alexander, R. (1989) *Changing Primary Practice*. Lewes: Falmer Press.

Alexander, R., Rose, J. and Woodhead, C. (1992) *Curriculum Organisation and Classroom Practice in Primary Schools*. London: DES.

Andersen, J. (1992) 'Quality in Early Childhood Education'. Paper presented at the European Educare Conference in Copenhagen, Denmark, October.

Andersson, B.E. (1990) 'Hur bra är egentligen dagis?' in Johansson, I. (1993) 'Quality in Early Childhood Education Services – What is That?' Paper presented at the Third European Conference on the Quality of Early Childhood Education, Thessaloniki, Greece, 1–3 September.

Anning, A. (1991) *The First Years at School*. Buckingham: Open University Press.

Ashman, A. and Conway, R. (1993) *Using Cognitive Methods in the Classroom*. London: Routledge.

Athey, C. (1990) *Extending Thought in Young Children*. London: Paul Chapman.

Atkin, J. (1991) 'Thinking about Play' in Hall, N. and Abbott, L. (eds), *Play in the Primary Curriculum*. London: Hodder & Stoughton.

Atkin, J., Bastiani, J. and Goode, J. (1988) *Listening to Parents: An Approach to the Improvement of Home–School Relations*. London: Cassell.

Baker, C. (1988) *Key Issues in Bilingualism and Bilingual Education*. London: Taylor & Francis.

Balageur, I., Mestres, J. and Penn, H. (1992) *Quality in Services for Young Children. A Discussion Paper*. London: European Commission Childcare Network.

Barrett, G. (1986) *Starting School: An Evaluation of the Experience.* London: Assistant Masters and Mistresses Association.

Bastiani, J. (ed.) (1988) *Parents and Teachers.* Slough: NFER/Nelson.

Bastiani, J. (1989) *Working with Parents: A Whole School Approach.* Windsor: NFER/Nelson.

Bennett, N. (1992) *Managing Learning in the Primary Classroom.* Stoke: Trentham Books.

Bennett, N. and Kell, J. (1989) *A Good Start? Four Year Olds in Infant Schools.* Oxford: Blackwell.

Beresford, E. (1992) 'The Politics of Parental Involvement' in Allen, G. and Martin, I. *Education and Community: The Politics of Practice.* London: Cassell.

Blenkin, G.M. and Kelly, A.V. (eds) (1992) *Assessment in Early Childhood Education.* London: Paul Chapman.

Braun, D. (1992) 'Working with Parents' in Pugh, G. (ed.), *Contemporary Issues in the Early Years.* London: Paul Chapman.

Breen, M. (1993) 'Coping with Babel: An Agenda for Language Education'. Inaugural Professorial Lecture, Edith Cowan University, Perth, Western Australia.

Brierley, J. (1987) *Give Me a Child Until He Is Seven.* Lewes: Falmer Press.

Broadfoot, P. (ed.) (1986) *Profiles and Records of Achievement. A Review of Issues and Practice.* London: Cassell.

Brown, S. and Cleave, S. (1991) *Early to School. Four Year Olds in Infant Classes.* Windsor: NFER/Nelson.

Browne, N. and France, P. (eds) (1986) *Untying the Apron Strings.* Milton Keynes: Open University Press.

Bruce, T. (1987) *Early Childhood Education.* Sevenoaks: Hodder & Stoughton.

Bruce, T. (1991) *Time to Play in Early Childhood Education.* Sevenoaks: Hodder & Stoughton.

Bruner, J.S. (1975) 'The Ontogenesis of Speech Acts', *Journal of Child Language,* 2: 1–19.

Bruner, J.S. (1980) *Under Five in Britain.* London: Grant McIntyre.

Bruner, J.S. (1983) *Child's Talk: Learning to Use Language.* Oxford: Oxford University Press.

Bruner, J.S. and Haste, H. (1987) *Making Sense. The Child's Construction of the World.* London: Methuen.

Calder, P. (1990a) 'The Training of Nursery Workers: The Need for a New Approach', *Children and Society,* 4(3): 251–60.

Calder, P. (1990b) 'Educare Can Advantage the Under Threes', in Rouse, D. *Babies and Toddlers: Carers and Educators, Quality for the Under Threes.* London: National Children's Bureau.

Central Advisory Council for Education (1963) *Half Our Future* (Newsom Report). London: HMSO.

Central Advisory Council for Education (1967) *Children and their Primary Schools* (Plowden Report). London: HMSO.

Cleave, S. and Brown, S. (1991) *Early to School: Four Year Olds in Infant Classes*. Windsor: NFER/Nelson.

Clift, P., Cleave, S. and Griffin, M. (1980) *The Aims, Roles and Deployment of Staff in the Nursery*. Slough: NFER.

Chazan, M., Laing, A.F., Jones, J., Harper, G.C. and Bolton, J. (1983) *Helping Young Children with Behaviour Difficulties*. London: Croom Helm.

Cowley, L. (1991) *Young Children in Group Day Care*. London: National Children's Bureau.

Curtis, A. and Hevey, D. (1992) 'Training to Work in the Early Years', in Pugh, G. (ed.), *Contemporary Issues in the Early Years*. London: Paul Chapman.

David, T. (1990) *Under Five – Under-educated*. Milton Keynes: Open University Press.

David, T. (ed.) (1993) *Educational Provision for our Youngest Children: European Perspectives*. London: Paul Chapman.

Department of Education and Science (1972) *A Framework for Expansion*. London: HMSO. Cmnd. 5174.

Department of Education and Science (1988) *A Survey of the Quality of Education for Four-Year-Olds in Primary Classes*. London: HMSO.

Department of Education and Science (1989a) *Discipline in Schools*. Report of the Committee of Enquiry chaired by Lord Elton. London: HMSO.

Department of Education and Science (1989b) *The Education of Children under Five*. HMI Aspects of Primary Education Series. London: HMSO.

Department of Education and Science (1990) *Starting with Quality: The Report of the Committee of Inquiry into the Quality of the Educational Experience Offered to 3- and 4-year-olds*. London: HMSO.

Department of Education and Science (1991) *Geography in the National Curriculum – Programme of Study*. London: HMSO.

Department of Education and Science (1992a) *The New Teacher in School*. London: HMSO.

Department of Education and Science (1992b) *Implementation of the curricular requirements of the Education Reform Act: Assessment, Recording and Reporting: A Report by HM Inspectorate on the 2nd Year, 1990–91*. London: HMSO.

Department of Education (Northern Ireland) (1993) *Review of Initial Teacher Training in Northern Ireland*. Report of Three Groups on Competences, Courses, Co-operation and ITT Structures, Co-ordination of ITT, Induction and In-service Training. Belfast: DENI.

Department of Health (1991) *The Children Act 1989 Guidance and Regulations. Vol. 2: Family Support. Day Care and Educational Provision for Young Children.* London: HMSO.

Dowling, M. (1992) *Education Three to Five.* London: Paul Chapman.

Drummond, M.J. (1990) 'The Child and the Primary Curriculum – From Policy to Practice', *The Curriculum Journal*, 2(2): 115–24.

Drummond, M.J. (1993) *Assessing Children's Learning.* London: David Fulton.

Drummond, M.J. and Nutbrown, C. (1992) 'Observing and Assessing Young Children', in Pugh, G. (ed.), *Contemporary Issues in the Early Years.* London: Paul Chapman.

Drummond, M.J., Lally, M. and Pugh, G. (eds) (1989) *Working with Young Children. Developing a Curriculum for the Early Years.* Nottingham: Nottingham Educational Suppliers, Arnold and National Children's Bureau.

Drummond, M.J., Rouse, D. and Pugh, G. (1992) *Making Assessment Work: Values and Principles in Assessing Young Children's Learning.* Nottingham: Nottingham Educational Suppliers, Arnold and National Children's Bureau.

Early Years Curriculum Group (1992) *First Things First. A Guide for Parents and Governors.* Litchfield: Boon Prints.

Edwards, C., Moorhouse, J. and Widlake, S. (1988) 'Language or English? The Needs of Bilingual Pupils', in Jones, M. and West, A. (eds), *Learning Me Your Language: Perspectives on the Teaching of English.* London: Mary Glasgow.

Edwards, V. and Redfern, A. (1988) *At Home in School: Parent Participation in Primary Education.* London: Routledge.

Eisenstadt, N. (1986) 'Parental Involvement: Some Feminist Issues', in Browne, N. and France, P. (eds), *Untying the Apron Strings.* Milton Keynes: Open University Press.

Epstein, D. and Sealey, A. (1990) *Where it Really Matters. Developing Anti-Racist Education in Predominantly White Schools.* Birmingham: Development Education Centre.

Evans, A. (1986) 'Pupil Profiles and Records of Achievement: An NUT Perspective', in Proudfoot, P. (ed.), *Profiles and Records of Achievement: A Review of Issues and Practice.* London: Cassell.

Ferri, E., Birchall, D., Gingell, V. and Gipps, C. (1981) *Combined Nursery Centres.* London: Macmillan.

Fulgham, R. (1986) *All I Really Need to Know I Learned in Kindergarten. Uncommon Thoughts on Common Things.* New York: Ivy Books.

Galvin, P., Mercer, S. and Costa, P. (1990) *Building a Better Behaved School.* London: Longman.

Gipps, C. (1990) *Assessment: A Teachers Guide to the Issues.* London: Hodder & Stoughton.

Hale, S. (1992) 'Starting School – Making Choices' in *Home School Partnerships in Oxfordshire*. Oxford LEA.

Hall, N. (1987) *The Emergence of Literacy*. Sevenoaks: Hodder & Stoughton, in association with the United Kingdom Reading Association.

Harvey, L. and Green, D. (1993) 'Defining Quality', *Assessment and Evaluation in Higher Education*, 18(1): 9–34.

Heaslip, P. (1987) 'Does the Glass Slipper Fit Cinderella? Nursery Teachers and their Training', in Clark, M.M., *Roles, Responsibilities and Relationships in the Education of the Young Child*. Occasional paper no. 13, *Educational Review*. Birmingham University.

Hennessy, E., Martin, S., Moss, P. and Melhuish, E. (1992) *Children and Day Care: Lessons from Research*. London: Paul Chapman.

Her Majesty's Inspectors (1987) *Good Behaviour and Discipline in Schools*. Education Observed No. 5. London: HMSO.

Hitchcock, G. (1986) *Profiles and Profiling: A Practical Introduction*. Harlow: Longman.

House of Commons Education, Science and Arts Committee (1988) *First Special Report. Educational Provision for the Under Fives*. HC 324, session 1988–89. London: HMSO.

Hurst, V. (1991) *Planning for Early Learning*. London: Paul Chapman.

Hurst, V. (1987) 'Parents and Professionals: Partnership in Early Childhood Education', in Blenkin, G.M. and Kelly, A.V. (eds), *Early Childhood Education: A Developmental Curriculum*. London: Paul Chapman.

Hutt, S.J., Tyler, S., Hutt, C. and Christopherson, H. (1989) *Play, Exploration and Learning*. London: Routledge.

ILEA (1986) *The Junior School Report, a Summary of the Main Report*. London: ILEA Research and Statistics Branch.

Isaacs, S. (1960) *Intellectual Growth in Young Children*. London: Routledge & Kegan Paul.

Johansson, I. (1993) 'Quality in early childhood services – what is that?' Paper presented at third European conference on the quality of early childhood education, 1–3 September, Thessaloniki, Greece.

Jowett, S., Baginsky, M., MacDonald MacNeil, M. (eds) (1991) *Building Bridges: Parental Involvement in Schools*. Slough: NFER/Nelson.

Karby, G. (1989) 'Children's Concept's of Their Own Play', in *The Voice of the Child*. London: Organisation Mondiale pour L'Education Prescolaire (OMEP) July Conference Proceedings.

Katz, L.G. (1993) 'Multiple Perspectives on the Quality of Early Childhood Programmes', *European Early Childhood Research Journal*, 1(2): 5–9.

Kelly, A. (1989) 'Education or Indoctrination? The Ethics of School-based Action Research', in Burgess, R. (ed.), *The Ethics of Educational Research*. London: Falmer Press.

Kelly, A.V. (1992) 'Concepts of Assessment: An Overview', in Blenkin, G.M. and Kelly, A.V. (eds), *Assessment in Early Childhood Education.* London: Paul Chapman.

Kinnock, G. and Millar, F. (1993) *By Faith and Daring.* London: Virago Press.

Kumar, V. (1993) *Poverty and Inequality in the UK. The Effects on Children.* London: National Children's Bureau.

Kyriacou, C. (1991) *Essential Teaching Skills.* Oxford: Basil Blackwell.

Laishley, J. (1983) *Working with Young Children.* London: Edward Arnold.

Lally, M. (1991) *The Nursery Teacher in Action.* London: Paul Chapman.

Lally, M. and Hurst, V. (1992) 'Assessment in Nursery Education: A Review of Approaches', in Blenkin, G.M. and Kelly, A.V. (eds), *Assessment in Early Childhood Education.* London: Paul Chapman.

Lassbo, G. (1993) 'The Third Step – An Attempt to Operationalize the Quality of Early Childhood Education in the Welfare State'. Department of Education and Educational Research. University of Gothenburg.

Leicester, M. (1989) *Multicultural Education: From Theory to Practice.* Windsor: NFER/Nelson.

Linden, J. (1993) *Child Development from Birth to Eight: A Practical Focus.* London: National Children's Bureau.

Manchester City Council Education Department (1990) *Profiling for Children of Primary School Age in Manchester Schools: A Practical Manual.* Manchester: City Council Education Department.

Manchester City Council Education Department (1992) *English for Children under Five Years of Age.* Manchester: City Council Education Department.

McCail, G. (1991) *Pre-five Environment Quality Rating Scale.* Edinburgh: Moray House.

McMillan, M. (1930) *The Nursery School.* London: Dent.

Meadows, S. (1993) *The Child As Thinker.* London: Routledge.

Meadows, S. and Cashdan, A. (1988) *Helping Children Learn.* London: David Fulton.

Melhuish, E. and Moss, P. (eds) (1990) *Day Care for Young Children: International Perspectives.* London: Routledge.

Montgomery, D. (1989) *Managing Behaviour Problems.* London: Hodder & Stoughton.

Mortimore, P., Sammons, P., Stoll, L. and Ecob, R. (1988) *School Matters: The Junior Years.* Wells: Open Books.

Moyles, J.R. (1989) *Just Playing? The Role and Status of Play in Early Childhood Education.* Milton Keynes: Open University Press.

Munby, S., Phillips, P. and Collinson, R. (1989) *Assessing and Recording Achievement.* Oxford: Basil Blackwell.

Munsch, R. (1982) *The Paper Bag Princess*. London: Hippo Books, Scholastic.

Murphy, R. (1991) 'National Developments in Primary School Assessments', in Harding, L. and Beech, J.R. (eds), *Educational Assessment of the Primary School Child*. Windsor: NFER.

National Association of Inspectors and Educational Advisers (1985) *The Needs of 3 to 5 Year Olds*. Letchworth: NAIEA.

National Commission (1993) *Learning to Succeed*. London: Heinemann.

National Curriculum Council (1990) *English Non-Statutory Guidance*. York: NCC.

National Primary Centre (1989) *Relationships*. Practical Issues in Primary Education No. 3. Oxford: National Primary Centre.

Northern Group of Advisers (1992) *Right from the Beginning: Assuring Quality in Early Education*. Gateshead: Publications Unit, Gateshead Metropolitan Borough Council Education Department.

Nias, J., Southworth, G. and Yeomens, R. (1989) *Staff Relationships in the Primary School*. London: Cassell.

Office for Standards in Education (OFSTED) (1993a) *Handbook for the Inspection of Schools*. London: HMSO.

Office for Standards in Education (OFSTED) (1993b) *First Class: The Standards and Quality of Education in Reception Classes*. London: HMSO.

Office for Standards in Education (OFSTED) (1993c) *Well Managed Classes in Primary Schools*. London: HMSO.

Opie, I. and Opie, P. (1959) *The Lore and Language of School Children*. Oxford: Clarendon Press.

Pascal, C. (1990) *Under Fives in Infant Classrooms*. Stoke: Trentham.

Piaget, J. (1968) *Six Psychological Studies*. London: University of London Press.

Pidgeon, S. (1992) 'Teacher Assessment through Record Keeping', in Blenkin, G.M. and Kelly, A.V. (eds), *Assessment in Early Childhood Education*. London: Paul Chapman.

Pollard, A. (1985) *The Social World of the Primary School*. London: Holt Education.

Pollard, A. and Tann, S. (1987) *Reflective Teaching in the Primary School: A Handbook for the Classroom*. London: Cassell.

Pugh, G. (ed.) (1992) *Contemporary Issues in the Early Years*. London: Paul Chapman.

Pugh, G. and De'Ath, E. (1989) *Working towards Partnership in the Early Years*. London: National Children's Bureau.

Purdon, L. (1993) 'An Exploration of the Potential of Structured Play for Early Writing with a Group of Five Year Old Children'. Unpublished independent curriculum study, The Manchester Metropolitan University.

Quinlan, P. (1990) *My Dad Takes Care of Me*. Annick Press: Canada.

Raychaudhuri, S. (1989) 'Children off the Edge – Language in the National Curriculum and the Bilingual Child', in *Language Matters*, No. 3. London: Centre for Learning in Primary Education.

Richman, N. and McGuire, J. (1988) 'Institutional Characteristics and Staff Behaviour in Day Nurseries', Children and Society, 2(2): 138–51.

Ritchie, R. (ed.) (1991) *Profiling in Primary Schools*. London: Cassell.

Rogers, C. (1951) *Client Centred Therapy*. Boston: Houghton Mifflin.

Rogers, C. (1969) *Freedom to Learn*. New York: Merrill.

Rouse, D. and Griffin, S. (1992) Quality for the under threes, in Pugh, G. (ed.) *Contemporary Issues in the Early Years*. London: P.C.P.

Royal Society of the Arts (1993) *Start Right. The Importance of Early Learning*. London: RSA.

Ruel, N. (1989) *Sharp-Eye Materials 'Me and Myself'*. Aylesbury: Ginn.

Salford Education Department (1990) *Assessment and Record Keeping in the Early Years*. Salford: Education Department.

Schaffer, H.R. (1992) 'Joint Involvement Episodes as Context for Development', in McGurk, H. (ed.), *Childhood Social Development*. Hove: Lawrence Erlbaum Associates.

Schools Examination and Assessment Council (1991) *Records of Achievement in Primary Schools*. London: HMSO.

Sheffield Education Department (1991) *Quality Criteria for Registration, Inspection and Review in Day Care and Education for Under Fives*. Sheffield: Education Department.

Sheffield LEA (1992) *Nursery Education. Guidelines for Curriculum, Organisation and Assessment*. Sheffield: Sheffield City Council.

Sugden, D. (ed.) (1989) *Cognitive Approaches to Special Education*. London: Falmer Press.

Sutton, R. (1991) *Assessment: A Framework for Teachers*. Windsor: NFER/Nelson.

Sylva, K., Roy, C. and Painter, M. (1980) *Childwatching at Playgroup and Nursery School* (Oxford Pre-School Research Project). Oxford: Grant McIntyre.

Sylva, K., Siraj-Blatchford, I. and Johnson, S. (1992) 'The Impact of the National Curriculum on Pre-School Practice', *The International Journal of Early Childhood* (OMEP), 24(1): 41–51.

Tizard, B. (1985) 'Social Relationships between Adults and Young Children, and Their Impact on Intellectual Functioning', in Hinde, R.A., Perret-Clermont, A.N. and Stevenson-Hinde, J. (eds), *Social Relationships and Cognitive Development*. Oxford: Oxford University Press.

Tizard, B. (1987) 'The Care of Young Children: Implications of Recent Research', in Clark, M.M. (ed.), *Roles, Responsibilities and Relationships in the Education of the Young Child*. Occasional Paper no. 13, *Educational Review*. University of Birmingham.

Tizard, B. and Hughes, M. (1984) *Young Children Learning*. London: Fontana.

Tyler, S. (1990) 'Play in Relation to the National Curriculum', in Hall, N. and Abbott, L. *Play in the Primary Curriculum*. Sevenoaks: Hodder & Stoughton.

Vygotsky, L.S. (1978) *Mind in Society: The Development of Higher Psychological Processes*. Cambridge, MA: MIT Press.

Vygotsky, L.S. (1986) *Thought and Language* (edited by A. Kozulin). Cambridge, MA: MIT Press.

Watt, J. (1987) 'Continuity in Early Childhood Education', in Clark, M.M. (ed.), *Roles, Responsibilities and Relationships in the Education of the Young Child*. Occasional Paper no. 13, *Educational Review*. University of Birmingham.

Webb, L. (1972) *Purpose and Practice in Nursery Education*. Oxford: Blackwell.

Wells, G. (1985) 'Language and Learning', in Wells, G. and Nicholls, J. (eds), *Language and Learning: An Interactional Perspective*. Lewes: Falmer Press.

Wetton, N. and Cansell, P. (1993) *Raising Self-esteem in the Primary School Classroom*. London: Forbes.

Wheldall, K. and Merrett, F. (1985) *Positive Teaching*. London: Unwin Books.

Willes, M. (1981) 'Children Becoming Pupils: A Study of Discourse in Nursery and Reception Classes', in Adelman, C., *Uttering, Muttering*. London: Grant McIntyre.

Wilson, A.N. (1978) *The Developmental Psychology of the Black Child*. New York: Africana Research Publishing.

Winter, R. (1991) 'Interviewers, Interviewees and the Exercise of Power (Fictional Critical Writing as a Method for Educational Research)', *British Educational Research Journal*, 17(3): 251–62.

Wood, D. (1988) *How Children Think and Learn*. Oxford: Basil Blackwell.

Woodhead, M. and McGrath, A. (eds) (1988) *Family, School and Society*. London: Hodder & Stoughton.

Wolfendale, S. (1992) *Empowering Parents and Teachers: Working for Children*. London: Cassell.

Yeomans, R. (1989) 'Sustaining a Partnership of Unequal Colleagues', *Early Years Journal*, 10(1): 26–8.

Index